WHAT OTHERS ARE SAYING ABOUT
Inside Church Planting Movements

"This fascinating book contributes to debates that focus on the question of CPMs reality. Having sat on the fence for years and imperiously granted a certain 'phenomenological being' to the reports of movements (including those emanating from my own country of birth), I found the author's honest scrutiny of CPM's reality, his evaluation of its critics/catalysts and his concise assessment of specific movements, refreshingly persuasive. The bonus for readers is in the author's invitation to imagine a path ahead which includes giving them the tools for independent assessments. I commend this book unreservedly to both the critics and advocates."

—Dr. David Emmanuel Singh
PhD Programme Director, Oxford Centre for Mission Studies

"A vital contribution to global missiology, Dave Garrison brings clarity, depth, and credibility to the conversation around Church Planting Movements. Grounded in 25 years of firsthand assessments, this book is both a challenge and a gift to anyone serious about multiplying disciples and churches across the nations."

—Alan Hirsch
Author of *The Forgotten Ways*,
Founder of Movement Leaders Collective

"*Inside Church Planting Movements* is a landmark contribution to the global missions conversation. Drawing from a rich archive of field research previously inaccessible to most, this book pulls back the curtain on one of the most discussed—and often misunderstood—phenomena of modern missions. With clarity, humility, and rigorous honesty, Garrison wrestles with the hard questions: Are Church Planting Movements real? Can we trust the reports? And how do we discern fact from fiction? This is essential reading for anyone serious about the Great Commission and eager to understand how God may be moving in our time."

—Wilson Geisler
Research Director, International Mission Board
of the Southern Baptist Convention

"Here he comes again! About twenty years ago, my friend David Garrison wrote a book *Church Planting Movements* that God used to inflame and influence the vision and practices of church planting movements worldwide. Now, in this groundbreaking research of 25 years, he takes us deep into the realities and contexts of church planting movements around the world and presents to the body of Christ a critical instrument that can be used to assess, learn and improve the quality of movements. I find this book not only a *must read* but also a *must study, reflect and apply* by every believer in Christ who is committed to see the advancement of God's kingdom through church planting movements."

—Dr. Bekele Shanko
Founder & President, Global Alliance
for Church Multiplication (GACX)

"Only David Garrison could distill thousands of pages of reports into a compelling story! From the pioneer who launched it all in the 1990s, this book brings you up to date on the exciting world of movements that are making disciples of Jesus among all nations. *Inside Church Planting Movements* is the data-rich resource we've been waiting for."

—WARRICK FARAH, Editor of *Motus Dei: The Movement of God to Disciple the Nations*

"David Garrison's *Inside Church Planting Movements* is a most honest look-in-the-mirror book that asks, "Are church planting movements *really* real?" Probing into 28 church movements with 25 years of solid qualitative and quantitative assessments, this book provides the critical insight into the depth and breadth, and the size and nature of church planting movements. Evidence demands a verdict! While confirming that real church planting movements exists—spanning continents from rural to urban areas, from the Buddhist to the Muslim to the Hindu world—this book also identifies the impediments that have derailed non-church planting movements. It also pinpoints the strategic adjustments that the "something-in-between" need to make to flourish into real church movements. Garnered from 25 years of hindsight, this book provides the insight and foresight needed for us to align with God's heart to unleash future church planting movements among the least reached so that all may hear."

—DR. MARY HO, International Executive Leader, All Nations International

"For two and a half decades, I have been a student of, practitioner in and around, and an academic voice advocating for "wonder" at the kairos moments of God in drawing people to Himself through the work of disciple-makers and church planters. Much ink has been spilled during that time on both sides of the issues surrounding movements. Sometimes advocates have over-promised and under-delivered on strategies. At other times, skeptics have wielded their criticism as a weapon as if the movements described in the Book of Acts were an anomaly bound to the First Century with little relevance for the Church that was birthed therein. But I agree with A.W. Tozer that, "Anything God has ever done, he can do now. Anything God has ever done anywhere, he can do here. Anything God has ever done for anyone, he can do for you." That sentiment has been, and remains, at the heart of David Garrison's research and writing, ever since he coined the term "church planting movements" over two decades ago. And in his most recent book on the subject, Garrison charitably evaluates and responds to both advocates and critics alike. This book is not merely a rehashing of old material. Rather, it is an honest look at the past and a hopeful look into the future of movement missiology. If advocates and critics alike would take the time to objectively read this book, senseless quarrels might dissipate. May Christ be honored and all who are far from God be brought near through faith-fueled obedience."

—Dr. George Robinson, Retired Professor of Missions, Southeastern Baptist Theological Seminary

"Veteran missiologist David Garrison provides an inspiring and reliable guide to honest and open methods of verification for Church Planting Movements (CPMs) among unreached peoples. This important research strengthens the reality of Christianity as a truly global religion where the vast majority of Christians are in the Global South."

—Todd Johnson, Distinguished Professor of Mission and Global Christianity, Gordon-Conwell Theological Seminary

"Talk of church planting movements simultaneously exhilarates and frustrates the missions community. Reactions range as wide as, "All of this is amazing! We should all be learning from them and seeking God to do the same in our ministries" to, "We should distrust and ward people away from church planting movements because they're deceptive and theologically weak!" But what's really happening? Why the polarization? Garrison's "Inside Church Planting Movements" allows readers a peek into the most exhaustive set of church planting movement assessments ever assembled. Without such assessments, we could blindly accept or reject all these incredible claims. After reading this book, you'll have presuppositions challenged, be encouraged by an organization's exhaustive efforts for integrity and insight, and have blinders removed to see the range of what's really happening in reported church planting movements."

—CHRIS CLAYMAN, Executive Director, Joshua Project

"Garrison offers a timely and insightful evaluation of Church Planting Movements (CPMs), balancing honest critique with thoughtful analysis. His work not only affirms the remarkable ways God is at work through CPMs today, but also challenges readers to consider how we assess and engage in these movements moving forward. With clarity and conviction, Garrison charts a course that is both encouraging and constructive—offering a valuable resource for practitioners, missiologists, and church leaders alike."

—DR. JAY MOON, Professor of Church Planting and Evangelism, Asbury Theological Seminary

"I have been a student of David Garrison for over 25 years. His writings on church planting movements opened the door and set the agenda for a generation. In his latest work, Inside Church Planting Movements, teams of assessors gathered data to reveal the size and nature of these movements. Are church planting movements real? In eleven of the case studies, the evidence was undeniable. He examines twenty-eight assessments of church planting movements over twenty-five years—from India to Cuba, from Guatemala to the megacities of China. Garrison explains how the assessments were done and provides the tools to help researchers conduct their own. This is a book for those who want to go beyond the hype of movements to the reality of what it takes to multiply disciples and churches to the glory of God."

—Steve Addison, Author of *Acts and the Movement of God*, Movements.net

"David Garrison's new book is a timely and valuable follow-up to his groundbreaking work on Church Planting Movements. I used the original in my classes at Liberty and Gateway, and I still refer to the 10 essentials in my teaching. This new volume continues that legacy—presenting data clearly, making insightful yet simple conclusions, and offering helpful assessment models. The categories—Confirmed CPMs, Non-CPMs, and those in between—are well presented and familiar. I especially appreciate the inclusion of diverse global players. This book is a fantastic resource for anyone teaching intercultural communication, evangelism, or missions. A truly helpful tool!"

—Dr. Eddie Pate, Senior Professor of Evangelism, Gateway Baptist Theological Seminary of the SBC

"*Inside Church Planting Movements* is the book we have been waiting for—a must-read for those interested in contemporary movements of the Spirit! I do not often write such words about books based on research findings. However, quality research is the Church's friend; and she has needed this friend over the past three decades. Skeptics and critics frequently stiff-armed any possibility of such healthy movements throughout the Majority World. Yet a handful of us knew in private what Garrison has now brought to the public: some reported movements were not movements at all; but many were indeed genuine—and even greater than what was recorded by missionaries! God has done and is doing some amazing things among the nations!"
—J.D. PAYNE, Chair of Christian Ministry, Samford University,
Author of *Discovering Church Planting*

"David Garrison's latest book should help to silence the all too often vitriolic criticism of church planting movements and disciple making movements. With grace and precision, Garrison examines movements around the globe according to the extensive data from one of the world's largest mission agencies, the IMB. Granted, while some of the data might be considered outdated it will no doubt cause critics to raise an unwarranted eyebrow. Nevertheless, Garrison's analysis of movement assessments demonstrates the depth of desire for movements to be theologically orthodox and ecclesiologically healthy. They are not immune to problems and, as a credible academic researcher, Garrison openly acknowledges such. Even so, he encourages the next generation of movement leaders to be equally meticulous in their assessments and provides a robust roadmap to guide the future of such endeavors."
—MICHAEL T. COOPER, PhD, Ephesiology Master Classes,
Kairos University, East West

"If evaluating church growth at home can be challenging, how much more so in diverse and difficult-to-access cross-cultural contexts! Garrison's well-informed overview of church movements helps us chart a course toward both faithfulness and fruitfulness in our Great Commission endeavors."

—STEVE RICHARDSON, President, Pioneers USA

"Have you heard that millions are coming to faith in Church Planting Movements (CPMs) and you are not convinced—but do not want to oppose God if these are happening? Or perhaps you are a movement practitioner who wants to be a more fruitful? This book with its careful analysis and practical tools can help.

As always, David asks the hard questions. His analysis of multiple movements on several continents is unflinching and provides evidence that 1) movements are real, far from perfect and yet consistent with biblical principles; 2) some movement reports are accurate (even low), some are not, some are mixed; and 3) audits provide hard data which can help teams make strategic adjustments.

This book, in addition to others (including the very first book on CPMs) is but the latest key contribution David has made toward making disciples of all *ethnê*. The excellent chapter on pioneering *"Coaches and Catalysts"* appropriately includes him in the list but greatly understates how greatly he has impacted the continuing growth of CPMs globally."

—DR. KENT PARKS, President and CEO, BEYOND

INSIDE CHURCH PLANTING MOVEMENTS

What 25 Years of
Assessments Reveal

David Garrison

P.O. Box 1884
Monument, CO 80132
www.churchplantingmovements.com/bookstore

Product Distribution: NoHutch@wigtake.org

Inside Church Planting Movements
© 2026 by WIGTake Resources

All rights reserved. No part of this publication may be reproduced in any form or by any means, electronic or print, without the prior written permission of the author, except in the case of brief quotations for review or critical articles.

ISBN: 978-1-939124-25-8

1. Missions. 2. Christianity. 3. Evangelism.
Garrison, David, 1957–

Scripture quotations, unless otherwise noted, are taken from the Holy Bible, New International Version®, NIV®. Copyright © 1973, 1978, 1984, 2011 by Biblica, Inc.® Used by permission of Zondervan. All rights reserved worldwide. www.zondervan.com. The "NIV" and "New International Version" are trademarks registered in the United States Patent and Trademark Office by Biblica, Inc.®

Scripture quotations marked ESV are taken from the ESV® Bible (The Holy Bible, English Standard Version®). Copyright © 2001 by Crossway, a publishing ministry of Good News Publishers. All rights reserved.
Cover Design by Matthew Simmons
Interior Design by Kristy L. Edwards
Copy Editor Maleah W. Bell
Author photo by Vickie Smith

Garrison, David
Inside Church Planting Movements

Printed in the United States of America

*To Sonia,
my lifelong partner, friend, and co-laborer
in this Great Commission adventure*

ANNOTATED TABLE OF CONTENTS

Preface .... *xvii*
Includes a rationale for the book, sources of information, the desired outcomes for the book, and a note regarding security constraints

PART ONE: MOVEMENTS, CRITICS, AND CATALYSTS
1. *What Are We Talking About?* 3
   Defines Church Planting Movements and Disciple Making Movements and their contrast from Insider Movements
2. *Why is this important?* 11
   Explains why both Church Planting Movements and their assessment are important
3. *The Critics Weigh In* 17
   Explores some of the more common objections to Church Planting Movements
4. *Catalysts and Coaches* 27
   Identifies agencies pursuing movements missiology and the growing number of movement practitioners, and catalysts of movements

Contents

PART TWO: MOVEMENTS AND THEIR ASSESSMENTS

5. *The First Church Planting Movements* 41
   Profiles the first four Church Planting Movements reported by missionaries of the International Mission Board between 2000 and 2005
6. *Communist, Berber, and Tribal Movements* 59
   Examines Church Planting Movements and their assessments that emerged in diverse and challenging contexts
7. *Can Church Planting Movements Occur in Cities?* 83
   Explores five urban movement assessments, including the largest Church Planting Movement in IMB history
8. *Yes, There Were Also Non-Movements* 103
   Provides examples that were reported to be movements but subsequently proved to be something else
9. *Muslim, Diaspora, and Hindu Movements* 125
   A look at three additional movements that posed unique challenges for assessment

PART THREE: THE ROAD AHEAD

10. *New Tools and Perspectives* 141
    Explores new tools that are emerging for examining Church Planting Movements
11. *Doing Your Own Assessment* 153
    Equips the reader to conduct their own Church Planting Movement assessment by walking through each of the steps involved
12. *Evidence that Demands a Verdict* 167
    Answers the book's fundamental questions, and derives lessons from the evidence produced by twenty-eight Church Planting Movement assessments
13. *Where Do We Go from Here?* 177
    Encourages readers to take up the challenge of catalyzing Church Planting Movements

Contents

APPENDICES: TOOLS YOU CAN USE

Appendix A: Refining Urban Assessments *183*
    An essay on the unique challenges of urban assessments
    and how to get them right

Appendix B: 2005 CPM Assessment Survey Instrument *187*
    The 2005 Church Planting Movement Assessment
    Guide developed by Dr. Jim Slack and the Global
    Research Department

Appendix C: 2022 CPM Assessment Survey Instrument *193*
    The 2022 Church Planting Movement Assessment
    process developed by Wilson Geisler and the IMB's
    Global Research Department

Appendix D: Seven Stages of a CPM Continuum *199*
    The Church Planting Movement Assessment Guide
    Continuum, edited by Stan Parks and Dave Coles

Bibliography *201*

Index *211*

Acknowledgments *215*

PREFACE

Church Planting Movements have sparked considerable debate since their emergence at the dawn of Christianity's third millennium. Some have viewed them as a Great Commission panacea, while others have dismissed them as illusory at best or sinister at worst.

If we pull back the curtain on Church Planting Movements, what will we find? Will this phenomenon prove to be a grand deception, akin to Dorothy's discovery when she peeked behind the curtain in Oz? Or will it prove to be as real as the wheat fields of Kansas?

This book addresses the question, Are Church Planting Movements real? If so, how do we know? How do we know when church multiplication has occurred? Can we trust what has been reported? And, if not, why not? How can we know the quality as well as the quantity of the work being reported? Can we really discern the truth from potential deception?

The research in this book draws from a number of sources. Chief among these is the extensive data found in the archives of the Southern Baptist International Mission Board (IMB). Between 1998 and 2022 the IMB collected thousands of pages of research drawn from twenty-eight onsite investigations into reported Church Planting Movements from Asia, Africa, Europe, and the Americas. This valuable trove of information has been inaccessible to the outside world—until now.

Just as important as the movements themselves are the ways in which they were assessed. Accordingly, much of this book will focus on "how we know what we know." Only as we learn how God is at work in these movements can we hope to clarify our own roles within them.

Wherever possible the actual names and locations of these movements have been retained. However, many of the movements occur in countries where rapid Christian growth remains imperiled. Those familiar with ministry among the world's least evangelized will understand the necessity of obscuring details in these security-sensitive contexts. In all cases, however, the facts and events recorded in this book are true to the best of the author's knowledge and ability.

David Garrison, PhD
Colorado 2025

PART ONE

MOVEMENTS, CRITICS, AND CATALYSTS

ONE

WHAT ARE WE TALKING ABOUT?

Since the founding of their denomination in 1845, Southern Baptists have focused on the task of world evangelization. Their efforts have grown considerably since then. By the end of the twentieth century the International Mission Board of the Southern Baptist Convention (IMB) was the largest Protestant denominational mission agency in the world. With 4,815 missionaries in 154 countries, supplemented by more than 30,000 volunteers and supported by 42,000 sending churches and an annual budget of $178.5 million, the IMB represented a significant portion of the world's evangelical mission force.

Each year IMB missionaries on mission fields around the world reported on the progress of their work. From rural villages in Africa to teeming cities in Asia, they tracked the number of new believers, baptisms, churches planted, and churches lost. These reports were reviewed by area directors before being submitted to the home office in Richmond, Virginia.[1] There, the IMB's Global Research Department compiled and scrutinized the data before presenting it to the IMB's seventy-seven trustees. Only after this extensive review process were the final statistics published as the IMB's *Annual Statistical Report* in the Southern Baptist Convention's *Book of Reports.*

The IMB's seventy-seven trustees represented the broad scattering of state conventions including Hawaii and Alaska. The majority of trustees were pastors serving a four-year term that could be renewed. They were vigilant in their oversight of the IMB's work and met as a full body six times per year. Yes, seventy-seven trustees from across the United States gathered every other month to oversee the agency's operations. Between plenary meetings, trustee committees and task forces collaborated with the IMB's nearly four hundred staff members who supported the growing overseas mission force.

The year 1999 was an unsettling one at the International Mission Board. The previous year, reports from four mission fields stood out. These reports were unusual. Rather than the typical count of one or two new church starts and a dozen or more baptisms, these four reports claimed thousands of newly baptized believers and hundreds of newly established churches. The extraordinary reports arrived from Latin America, East Asia, South Asia, and Southeast Asia.

The report from a Latin American country indicated a decade of growth from 229 churches in 1989 to a staggering 3,258 churches in 1998. The East Asian report described a ministry that had begun in 1993 with only two churches but had increased

---

1. The *Annual Statistical Report* of the International Mission Board is published annually in the Southern Baptist Convention's *Book of Reports*. The 2000 edition can be accessed online at: http://media2.sbhla.org.s3.amazonaws.com/annuals/SBC_Annual_2000.pdf. The 2000 *Annual Statistical Report* was 38 pages in length and provided data in 123 categories ranging from personnel count and evangelism to human needs ministries and media ministries.

to 550 churches in 1998. The South Asian work, which began in 1989 with 28 churches, had risen to 2,000 churches in 1998. The Southeast Asian ministry, which began in 1990 with approximately 600 believers, had risen to more than 60,000 by the end of the decade. If these reports were true, then something out of the ordinary was happening.[2]

Upon receiving these extraordinary reports, the IMB's Global Research Department reached out to regional leaders to verify their accuracy. The regional supervisors assured them, though unusual, the reports appeared to be legitimate. The missionaries responsible for these reports were experienced veterans who confidently vouched for the veracity of their statistics.

In 1998 I was serving as the IMB's associate vice president with responsibility for overseeing the Global Research Department and the Annual Statistical Report. In early 1999 I gathered a team of missionaries and staff researchers to investigate further. We asked critical questions: What is happening here? Are these numbers accurate? What do they have to teach us? How can we be sure? In March of that year we convened a second group of missionaries in Singapore to explore the same questions.

In October 1999 I compiled our findings into a fifty-seven-page booklet titled *Church Planting Movements*.[3] The booklet analyzed the reported movements and sought to extract meaningful insights. Though originally published by the IMB for internal use, the booklet sparked widespread interest, leading to

---

2. Each of these reports is described in greater detail in the author's booklet, *Church Planting Movements* (Richmond, VA: IMB, 1999).

3. The fifty-seven-page booklet *Church Planting Movements* (1999) is available as a free download at: https://churchplantingmovements.com/free-booklets, accessed August 9, 2024.

thousands of copies distributed in English, and its further translation into more than forty languages.[4]

We were seeing something new, and we wanted to describe it accurately. Rather than embellish the phenomenon with theological speculation or exaggerated claims, we adhered to a strictly descriptive definition. Based on the four movement case studies, we defined Church Planting Movements as the rapid and multiplicative increase of indigenous churches planting churches within a given people group or population segment.[5]

As Church Planting Movements spread into other mission agencies, some modified the definition to reflect their own priorities and sensibilities. Some agencies inserted "biblical" before "churches" in their definition, hinting at criticisms they were already anticipating. Others drew from 2 Timothy 2:2, emphasizing the importance of four generations of reproduction as a defining feature.[6] Regardless of the specific terminology, each of these definitions seemed to describe the same phenomenon: not merely church planting, nor the incremental addition of churches, but rather a rapid multiplication of indigenous churches.

In the years that followed, other terms were coined. One of the most popular was Disciple Making Movements (DMMs), first circulated by former IMB missionary David Watson. While both the IMB and Watson saw church multiplication as their desired outcome, the IMB was more explicit on the importance of planting churches while Watson zeroed in on the primary task of making disciples. Watson contended that if disciples were

---

4. Each of these non-English translations of the booklet was produced by local initiatives without subsidy or initiative of the International Mission Board.

5. Garrison, *Church Planting Movements*, 7.

6. "And the things you have heard me say in the presence of many witnesses entrust to reliable people who will also be qualified to teach others" (2 Tim 2:2).

What Are We Talking About?

made in accordance with Jesus's Great Commission (Matthew 28:19–20), churches would naturally follow.[7]

Some years later a parallel idea circulated through the mission world called Insider Movements (IMs). Insider Movements were defined as "any movement to faith in Christ where a) the gospel flows through pre-existing communities and social networks, and where b) believing families, as valid expressions of the Body of Christ, remain inside their socioreligious communities, retaining their identity as members of that community while living under the Lordship of Jesus Christ and the authority of the Bible."[8]

While the terms Church Planting Movements (CPMs) and Disciple Making Movements (DMMs) are often used interchangeably, Insider Movements differed significantly. While Insider Movements may lead to Church Planting Movements, the essence of CPMs is multiplying churches comprised of new believers. By contrast, because Insider Movements "remain inside their socioreligious communities," they may lack the presence of identifiable churches. For this reason Insider Movements are more difficult to evaluate; they often remain anonymous or hidden within a non-Christian community. The purpose of this book is neither to critique nor explore Insider Movements. Our focus is on Church Planting Movements.

At the heart of Church Planting Movements, of course, is "identifiable churches." Did the IMB have a clear understanding of what constitutes a church, or did they leave it to their four thousand missionaries to arrive at their own definitions? In fact,

---

7. In addition to his website, https://www.contagiousdiciplemaking.com, Watson published his DMM (Disciple Making Movements) missiology in the book he co-authored with his son Paul, *Contagious Disciple Making: Leading Others on a Journey of Discovery* (Nashville: Thomas Nelson, 2014).

8. Rebecca Lewis, "Promoting Movements to Christ within Natural Communities," *International Journal of Frontier Missions*, 24:2 (Summer 2007): 75–76, http://www.ijfm.org/PDFs_IJFM/24_2_PDFs/24_2_Lewis.pdf.

the IMB was quite prescriptive on this point. Prior to 2005, in the IMB's instructions to their missionaries for completing the Annual Statistical Report, missionaries were given this clear definition of a church:

> A local church is a group of baptized believers covenanted together into community by the Holy Spirit for the purpose of worship, fellowship, witness, nurture and ministry. The following characteristics are considered when completing the statistical report:
>
> 1. Meet regularly for worship, fellowship, mutual support and ministry.
> 2. Proclaim Christ to unbelievers and disciple believers.
> 3. Organize and administer their affairs, choosing their leadership (who may or may not be paid, trained, ordained, or one of the members of the group).
> 4. Administer the ordinances of baptism and the Lord's Supper.[9]

After 2005 the IMB clarified further their definition of a church to ensure its alignment with Southern Baptists' newly adopted 2000 Baptist Faith and Message as follows:

> A New Testament church of the Lord Jesus Christ is an autonomous local congregation of baptized believers, associated by covenant in the faith and fellowship of the gospel; observing the two ordinances of Christ, governed by His laws, exercising the gifts, rights, and privileges invested in them by His Word, and seeking to extend the gospel to the ends of the earth.

---

9. Provided to the author by the Global Research Department of the International Mission Board, SBC.

What Are We Talking About?

Each congregation operates under the Lordship of Christ through democratic processes. In such a congregation each member is responsible and accountable to Christ as Lord. Its scriptural officers are pastors and deacons. While both men and women are gifted for service in the church, the office of pastor is limited to men as qualified by Scripture.[10]

While each of the world's more than 45,000 denominations will have its own definition of a church, these are the ones that shaped the evaluative filters of the IMB assessments provided in this book. Perhaps the most important takeaway from these definitions is that they were shared universally by the IMB's missionaries and movement assessors. Church planting was a core function of IMB missionaries, and they had no tolerance for arbitrariness or ambiguities on that subject.

Today, Church Planting Movements are studied, debated, and pursued around the world. At the end of the twentieth century, however, they were the subject of some concern in the halls of the International Mission Board. How could staff explain the rapid multiplication of new churches to its trustees—most of whom were pastors who had never planted a church themselves?

It was these questions that prompted the IMB to conduct its first CPM assessments in the year 2000. Before we dive into those assessments, let's take a moment to ask why Church Planting Movements are important, and why it is important to evaluate them.

---

10. Global Research Department, SBC.

TWO

WHY IS THIS IMPORTANT?

Why are Church Planting Movements important, and why is it important to assess them?

The Importance of CPMs

Two factors frame the importance of Church Planting Movements. These factors are lostness and population growth.

Let's begin with lostness. Christians believe that people are lost without a redemptive relationship with Jesus Christ. If a person does not share this belief, then any discussion about the importance of CPMs is irrelevant. However, for those who do believe that the gospel is essential to eternal salvation, Church Planting Movements, which are claiming thousands of new believers, are of great significance.

The second factor is population growth. Each year the world adds 83 million souls to its population (think two Canadas each year!).[1] Viewed from the other side of life's spectrum, 60 million

---

1. United Nations, Department of Economic and Social Affairs, "World Population projected to reach 9.8 billion in 2050, and 11.2 billion in 2100," https://www.un.org/development/desa/en/news/population/world-population-prospects-2017.html#:~:text=With%20roughly%2083%20million%20people%20being%20added%20to,assuming%20that%20fertility%20levels%20will%20continue%20to%20decline, accessed Oct 30, 2024.

people die each year—at least 41 million of whom have no relationship with Jesus Christ or his Church.[2] Tunneling down further, *every day* more than 112,000 souls pass into eternity with no relationship to Jesus Christ.

Perhaps the exponential nature of population growth, more than any other objective fact, underscores the importance of Church Planting Movements. While each individual conversion and each new church plant is valuable, if these new believers and churches are not also multiplying exponentially, then their incremental increases are simply falling further and further behind the world's relentless population growth.

Rapidly multiplying churches of new disciples not only keep pace with the global population growth, they often exceed it. This characteristic of Church Planting Movements sets it apart from other forms of evangelistic outreach and traditional church planting.

At their core Church Planting Movements combine gospel proclamation with church formation. While evangelism alone leads to individual decisions to follow Christ, it is within churches that ongoing growth in Christ takes place. This synergy of evangelism with church formation is what makes Church Planting Movements so critical to Christian aspirations to reach a world in need of the gospel.

Church Planting Movements are important if we believe forty-one million souls transition into eternity each year without Christ. Church Planting Movements are important if we believe churches are the communities through which new disciples mature in their relationship with Christ. Thus, Church Planting Movements are vitally important to every Christian who wishes

---

2. See "The World Counts," at https://www.theworldcounts.com/populations/world/deaths, accessed October 30, 2024. In 2024, 31.6% of the world's population professed some form of Christianity.

Why Is This Important?

to extend Christ's kingdom into the world's rapidly growing population and see the fulfillment of the Great Commission.

The Importance of Assessments

Let's be honest—Church Planting Movements could be a fabrication. Simply put, people lie; and, more graciously, people make mistakes. But why would missionaries lie? you may ask. A critical eye would simply follow the money. Hundreds of millions of dollars flow from individual Christians through churches and mission agencies each year with the express aim of fulfilling the Great Commission. Better stories often lead to better giving appeals.

Generous Christians want to make an eternal impact and advance Christ's kingdom. Donors ask, "What is the impact of my giving?" While Christian institutions in less hostile lands can easily show the return on investment of the funds they receive— new buildings constructed, ongoing ministries funded—Church Planting Movements typically occur in more hostile settings, where it is more difficult to record and report results. Yet, as we will see, these are the environments in which most CPMs are taking place.

The opaque nature of CPM reports has led many Christian donors to restrict their contributions to ministries where "hard numbers" can be provided. This is no small matter. As Forbes Magazine reports, "Baby Boomers . . . are expected to transfer $30 trillion in wealth to younger generations. . . . In no prior time in the history of America has such a vast amount of wealth moved through the hands of generations."[3]

---

3. Mark Hall, "The Greatest Wealth Transfer in History," *Forbes* magazine online, https://www.forbes.com/sites/markhall/2019/11/11/the-greatest-wealth-transfer-in-history-whats-happening-and-what-are-the-implications/?sh=2d9e5da74090, accessed April 20, 2024.

Assessments of movements address the concerns of donors who care about the stewardship of their gifts. Without thorough assessments, conscientious donors will continue to direct their giving to recipients who are capable of providing audited reports, while strategically important movements in data-poor environments will continue to languish in darkness. How can the church give if it does not know? And how can it know unless the work is assessed?

A Look in the Mirror

Even more important than the concerns of donors are the needs of those on the mission field. Both the missionary church planters and, even more so, the new believers and churches being planted need to understand what is happening in their midst. Assessments hold up a mirror to the emerging movements and allow them to see where God is at work, how he is working, and how they can best contribute. Good Church Planting Movement assessments identify where the church is and where it is not; where it is healthy and where it needs help. Let's look at some examples.

A South Asian Church Planting Movement was reporting remarkable growth with hundreds of new churches and thousands of baptisms. There was little doubt that God was doing something substantial among this people group. However, a Church Planting Movement assessment revealed that the vast majority of the people in this movement were nonliterate and had never seen a Bible in their own language. Even if they had seen one, they could not have read it, as their language was primarily oral. As a result of the assessment, missionaries and their partners imported audio cassettes and micro-SD cards containing the Bible in their heart language.

Why Is This Important?

The assessment provided a lens through which the movement participants could see deficiencies that would soon have produced significant problems. As a result of the assessment, the movement's leaders were able to develop creative solutions to infuse biblical guidance into the movement as it continued to grow.

In another example, nearly 100,000 Muslims had come to Christ in a relatively short period of time. A Church Planting Movement assessment confirmed the size of the movement and everyone rejoiced, but something was wrong. The vast majority of those who had come to Christ were men—specifically literate men. Closer scrutiny revealed that this was primarily a men's movement to Christ.

The assessment revealed that the gender segregation of the Islamic community had carried over into the movement itself. Men were winning men to Christ but failing to spread the good news to their wives, mothers, daughters, or sisters. The Church Planting Movement assessment revealed the dark cloud behind the silver lining. Upon seeing the problem the missionaries and their local partners began strategizing how to reach the largely nonliterate women in their communities. The result was an awakening among the Muslim women who responded warmly to the message.

Church Planting Movements are important, and their assessments help us better understand them. However, not everyone holds these movements in high regard, as we will see in our next chapter.

THREE

THE CRITICS WEIGH IN

When a friend first learned there were opponents to Church Planting Movements, he responded with surprise. "How could anyone object to Church Planting Movements?" As a fellow skeptic I could only reply, "It's what we do."

While critics of CPMs have been numerous, their objections often fall into a few distinct categories, and we'll examine eight of them in this chapter. It is important to note that identifying these criticisms is not to impugn the integrity of those who have voiced them but rather to help the reader understand better the issues they have raised.

In this chapter we will resist the temptation to try to resolve each criticism presented. Instead, we will attempt to present critics' concerns fairly, with measured responses. Afterwards, though, we encourage the reader to filter these criticisms through the evidence found in the twenty-eight movements and their assessments. Only then, on the basis of evidence, will we be able to accurately evaluate the issues that movement critics have raised.

1. Denominational Critics

During a CPM training event, a mission administrator objected to the idea of rapidly multiplying, lay-led house churches. He protested, "Our missionaries are commissioned to start Reformed churches!" His frank objection captured a broader sentiment shared by many within denominational mission circles. One could easily replace "Reformed" with "Baptist" or "Pentecostal" or a number of other denominational markers.

Certainly not all denominational sending agencies are opponents of Church Planting Movements. However, when movements rapidly reproduce new believers, disciples, and churches without expressing the denominational identity of the missionaries who catalyzed them, it may raise questions on the home front. Western denominations that are deeply invested in their own history are not wrong to ask whether or not these new churches share the values of their tradition. But the hard truth is that the majority of these movements do not see denominational identity at the core of what God is doing among them.

In Church Planting Movements, denominational identity often fades into the background, eclipsed by less complicated norms, such as fidelity to biblical authority.

2. Seminary Critics

While some Christian seminaries include notable advocates of CPMs, others within their ranks warn that without solid theological education Church Planting Movements are doomed to heretical detours. As one seminary professor dismissingly commented, "A heretical movement is still heretical." But are Church Planting Movements heretical? Assessments can provide answers.

It is true that the rapidly multiplying churches in Church

The Critics Weigh In

Planting Movements tend to rely upon nonprofessional, lay-led leaders. Because CPM church leaders are often employed in secular vocations, they gravitate toward education in smaller, manageable segments. Theological training is there, but it is typically provided through decentralized "just-in-time training," rather than lengthy, formal seminary degrees.

Instead of seeing this as a conflict between movements and seminaries, it is possible to see the potential for a new kind of partnership. Innovative seminaries are rising to the challenge by offering online courses and theological education by extension in various languages. These seminaries offer fresh avenues for training that align with the needs of rapidly multiplying disciples and churches, often in areas where formal theological institutions are scarce or even illegal.

3. Reformed Critics

The Reformed tradition has long been a cornerstone of Protestant theology, with John Calvin's work (1536–64) shaping church structures that have endured for centuries. In fact, many exemplary catalysts of Church Planting Movements are themselves Reformed, yet the movements they catalyze often do not adhere to the ecclesiological prescriptions of their Reformation tradition.

One of the most outspoken Reformed critics of Church Planting Movements is Dr. Mark Dever, pastor of Capitol Hill Baptist Church in Washington DC., and founder of the 9Marks Network. In a 2019 interview Dever condemned Church Planting Movements, ascribing to them:

> Lots of fake statistics. . . . They are sloppy in defining what a church is. And ultimately when you're sloppy in defining

what a church is, you're going to be sloppy in defining what a Christian is. And people will go to hell because of your errors. So, I take their motives as good. I take their work as sinister.[1]

To better understand Dever's concerns, we should examine his definition of a healthy church. According to the 9Marks Network, the first mark of a healthy church is "expositional preaching."[2] Expository preaching, while highly valued in the evangelical world, requires years of formal education, something rarely found in Church Planting Movements. Church Planting Movements typically begin with participative, lay-led discovery Bible study engagement of Scripture.

The ninth mark of a healthy church, according to Dever's paradigm, is "a plurality of elders to shepherd the church."[3] Shared leadership provides the church with a system of checks and balances and ensures its optimal navigation through complex decisions. While plural leadership is not unusual in rapidly multiplying Church Planting Movements, finding "elders" from movements of new disciples is practically an oxymoron.

The absence of these two defining marks in Church Planting Movements explains why Dr. Dever would denounce them and their advocates as "sinister." The legitimate core of Dr. Dever's concern would appear to be that these movements could result in dubious believers who could easily fall prey to heresy or apostasy. However, this hypothesis needs to be tested. Onsite assessments provide us with a means of testing, and when needed, correcting errors.

---

1. Mark Dever, interview by Brooks Buser, "Mark Dever on Church Planting Movements," YouTube, October 16, 2019, https://www.youtube.com/watch?v=fi9Xp8D7_Oc.

2. See the 9 Marks at: https://www.9marks.org/about/, accessed June 16, 2025.

3. 9 Marks at: https://www.9marks.org/about/, accessed June 16, 2025.

The Critics Weigh In

A further 9Marks criticism of Church Planting Movements has been lumped under the charge of pragmatism. 9Marks authors Andy Johnson and Matt Rhodes argue that Church Planting Movement missionaries have adopted a slavish addiction to results at the expense of biblical fidelity.[4]

The charge of slavish addiction to results seems harsh at best. Missionaries are problem solvers, but they are biblical problem solvers. As we will see in the case studies that follow, catalysts of Church Planting Movements share with their Reformed critics a deep commitment to biblical authority. In healthy Church Planting Movements, missionaries endeavor to sow scriptural fidelity into the very DNA of each reproducing church. Assessments allow us to examine the DNA of the churches in movements to determine whether or not this commitment to biblical authority is alive and well.

In fact, Church Planting Movement assessments were developed for the very purpose of investigating the objections that critics have raised. As they have examined both the quantity and quality of these movements, CPM assessments have discovered there are numerous ways for the church to submit to the authority of Scripture, feed the sheep, and shepherd the flock.

In response to Western critics, defenders of Church Planting Movements often point to the evidence of the churches themselves. Comparing churches in movements with traditional Western churches, they ask, "Which most closely resemble the churches we find in the New Testament?" CPM assessments provide us with tangible information to answer that question.

---

4. See Andy Johnson, "Pragmatism, Pragmatism, Everywhere!" in the *9Marks Journal*, February 26, 2010, https://www.9marks.org/article/pragmatism-pragmatism-everywhere/; and Matt Rhodes, *No Shortcut to Success: A Manifesto for Modern Missions* (Wheaton, IL: Crossway, 2021).

4. Landmarkist Critics

The distinctly nineteenth-century Baptist heresy of Landmarkism is rarely highlighted today, but many of its ideas continue to permeate conservative churches and mission efforts.[5] When critics raise objections to baptisms being conducted by non-ordained leaders, they are echoing the hierarchical doctrine of the church espoused in Landmarkism.

The Landmarkist heresy teaches that only churches connected to the ancient stream of true churches (by which they mean certain Baptist churches) are legitimate churches, and only true churches are ordained by God to conduct baptism and Communion. However, the Landmarkist insistence upon clergy ordination by a "true church" has proven unable to keep pace with rapidly multiplying new disciples and churches. Church Planting Movements, by contrast, are driven by the laity, emphasizing the priesthood of every believer. Thus, CPMs typically encourage baptism upon conversion, often by the person who led the new believer to faith.

5. Ministry as Mission Critics

In the New Testament, ministry (*diakonia*) means service, but service to whom? Ministry to other Christians, though a valid Christian virtue, is not the same as pioneering missions. Pioneering missions often includes and even depends upon ministry, but it prioritizes evangelism and church planting among unreached non-Christians.

---

5. See, for example, the Cuban movement in chapter 6 below. On Southern Baptist's break with Landmarkism, see James Leo Garrett Jr., *Baptist Theology: A Four-Century Study* (Macon, GA: Mercer University Press, 2009), 213.

The Critics Weigh In

In recent years Western churches have increasingly confused ministry among overseas Christian communities with missions, resulting in a trajectory that falls short of engaging unreached non-Christian populations. The church's mission drift from pioneering evangelism and church planting to ministry among overseas Christians has coincided with the rise of short-term mission trips. These cross-cultural volunteers build church buildings, establish orphanages, offer theological training, and minister to those in need. While all of these ministries are laudable, they rarely lead to Church Planting Movements.

Church Planting Movements among unreached non-Christians call for a different sort of engagement. They require years of investment in language and culture, investments that are often beyond the reach of short-term ministers, with the result that many of these short-term ministers are left feeling marginalized and ambivalent about Church Planting Movements.

6. Missionary Critics

Since the late eighteenth century, Protestant churches have deployed hundreds of thousands of missionaries to virtually every corner of the globe. These missionaries have contributed immensely to the spread of the gospel. At the same time, the vast majority of them have never seen a Church Planting Movement.

Perhaps it is not surprising, then, that some of these missionaries have questioned the very existence of Church Planting Movements and dismissed them as fraudulent or shortcuts to a questionable end.[6] To their credit, though, others have viewed Church Planting Movements as an answer to prayer, the result

---

6. See Rhodes, *No Shortcut to Success*.

of decades of learning how to catalyze indigenous and rapidly multiplying believers, disciples, and churches.

7. Critics of Rapid Multiplication

One of the earliest objections to the descriptive definition of Church Planting Movements was its inclusion of the word *rapid*. Rapidity has been equated with immaturity, invoking Jesus's parable of the sower in which some seeds "sprang up quickly," but "withered because they had no root" (Matt. 13:5-6).

Missionaries engaged in movements are quick to acknowledge that maturation in Christ is anything but rapid. It is a lifelong process of growing in Christlikeness. Maturation in Christ, however, is not a prerequisite for obedience to Christ, and these movement catalysts do stress immediate obedience to Christ. Immediate obedience fuels indigenous evangelism that spreads rapidly through familial relationships. CPM assessments have revealed two intrinsic factors leading to rapid multiplication.

The first factor the assessments discovered was a sharp awareness among these new disciples that their family and friends were lost without the saving message of the gospel. This passionate conviction provoked in these new Christians an urgent desire to share their newfound faith.

A second more mundane factor that assessments unearthed was related to the size limitations of the house churches found in these movements. As new believers filled a small apartment or house church, it quickly became necessary for them to hive off new believers to other homes, thus rapidly multiplying new house churches.

Simply put, new disciples and churches in CPMs multiplied rapidly, not because missionaries demanded it, or because they were instantly becoming mature Christians, but because they had to—their passionate evangelism and restrictive house-church size necessitated it.

8. "Why So Remote?" Critics

Some critics have asked why CPMs always seem to occur in restricted, hostile regions where they are difficult to observe. If Church Planting Movements were more prevalent in the West, they argue, they would appear less alien and incredible.

It is true that Church Planting Movements thrive in places where Christianity is persecuted. In fact, when churches are free to meet in formal buildings with well-trained clergy they tend to do so. When legal constraints and societal pressures exist, churches find creative solutions, often meeting in homes or informal venues, giving rise to Church Planting Movements.

In the chapters ahead we will explore case studies of Church Planting Movements and their assessments, and as we do so we will keep in mind the objections that sincere critics have raised. Along the way, we will note the efforts missionaries are making to determine the actual quality as well as the quantity of churches found within them. Before we do, though, let's look at some of the key agencies and individuals who are contributing to the spread of movements throughout the world today.

FOUR

CATALYSTS AND COACHES

While it is not possible to identify everyone who has contributed to the spread of Church Planting Movements, this chapter will highlight some of the pioneering individuals and agencies that have self-identified as CPM aspirants and catalysts.

An important disclaimer is needed here. Missionaries are strong individuals, which means just because their agency embraces the vision of Church Planting Movements, it doesn't mean every missionary in that agency is actively pursuing the same vision. More common are those individuals within mission agencies who have catalyzed Church Planting Movements, much to the surprise and delight, or even chagrin, of their sending body.

Agencies and Networks

A look through the "Directory of North American Agencies" in the *North American Mission Handbook: US and Canadian Protestant Ministries Overseas 2017–2019*[1] is revealing. The

---

1. Peggy E. Newell, ed., "Directory of North American Agencies," *North American Mission Handbook: US and Canadian Protestant Ministries Overseas 2017-2019*, 22nd ed. (Pasadena, CA: William Carey Library, 2017).

Handbook lists fifty-four North American agencies that explicitly state that Church Planting Movements or Disciple Making Movements are core to their organizational purpose. Some of these agencies include:

1. AIMS
2. Anglican Frontier Missions
3. Asian Access
4. Baptist International Outreach
5. BEYOND
6. Christar Canada
7. Communitas International
8. Crossover Communications International
9. East-West Ministries International
10. Eastern Mennonite Missions
11. Foursquare Missions International
12. Frontiers
13. Global Frontier Missions
14. Global Gates
15. Greater Europe Mission
16. IMB of the Southern Baptist Convention
17. OMF International
18. One Challenge
19. Pioneers
20. RP (Reformed Presbyterian) Global Missions
21. TEAM Expansion
22. WEC International

... and many more.

However, the *Handbook* list is limited to North American agencies and doesn't account for the many movement-oriented efforts emanating from the growing ranks of non-Western agencies. Even within the North American context there are numerous agencies and churches with significant investments in Church Planting Movements that never bothered to update their organizational profile in the *Handbook's* directory. For example, the *Handbook* fails to mention the considerable

CPM contributions by missionaries serving with such North American agencies as the Assemblies of God's Live Dead,[2] New Generations,[3] Youth With a Mission (YWAM),[4] Biglife,[5] OM (Operation Mobilization),[6] e3 Partners,[7] Cru,[8] the Christian and Missionary Alliance,[9] Lutheran Church Missouri Synod,[10] Final Command Ministries,[11] and others.

Many other agencies have been invaluable contributors to Church Planting Movements, even though their purpose statements do not reflect their contributions. Among these

---

2. See Live Dead's FAQ on Church Planting Movements at https://www.livedead.org/faqs/, accessed June 26, 2024.

3. See New Generations website, https://newgenerations.org, accessed June 24, 2025.

4. YWAM is involved in virtually every area of mission and ministry in virtually every corner of the globe, so it is not surprising that many YWAM missionaries pioneer and collaborate with CPM ministries.

5. "Biglife trains believers to make disciples of Jesus, leading to disciple-making movements." See Biglife Global, https://big.life, accessed June 26, 2024.

6. With their focus on the unreached, evangelism, and literature distribution, OM missionaries have been a part of many Church Planting Movements, even though this is not a focus of their ministry. See https://www.omusa.org, accessed June 26, 2024.

7. See "Multiplying disciples and churches across the globe until every person & place has been reached for Christ," e3 Partners, https://e3partners.org, accessed May 11, 2025.

8. Cru, formerly Campus Crusade for Christ, is historically known more for evangelism and campus ministry than Church Planting Movements. However, their Vice President for Global Church Movements, Bekele Shanko, is also the leader of GACX (Global Alliance for Church Multiplication), a coalition of 108 agencies and churches with a vision to see "a healthy, multiplying, and sustainable church for every 1000 people on earth." See GACX , https://gacx.io/about/mission-vision-values, accessed June 26, 2024.

9. While the Christian and Missionary Alliance (C&MA) does not explicitly state that Church Planting Movements are its purpose, its field missionaries in Southeast Asia are among the most prolific Church Planting Movement catalysts in the region.

10. Like the C&MA, the Lutheran Church Missouri Synod does not explicitly aspire to Church Planting Movements; however, this has not stopped some of their missionaries from catalyzing them in Asia.

11. See "Catalyze Disciple Making Movements," Final Command Ministries, https://www.finalcommand.com, accessed May 11, 2025.

are Wycliffe Bible Translators,[12] GalCom International[13] and MegaVoice,[14] the Timothy Initiative,[15] SIL (Summer Institute of Linguistics),[16] the JESUS Film Project,[17] SEED Company,[18] Faith Comes By Hearing,[19] Every Home for Christ,[20] the Joshua Project,[21] and Global Recordings.[22] Beyond these are numerous churches and independent missionaries around the world who are pursuing Church Planting Movements and Disciple Making Movements without ever recording their work in a mission directory.

---

12. Learn more from Wycliffe Bible Translators at https://www.wycliffe.org, accessed June 26, 2024.

13. GalCom draws its name from the ministry's origins in the Galilee and from the Hebrew for the word for commit. GalCom provides solar-powered, fix-tuned radios widely used to communicate the gospel among unreached people groups. Learn more at Galcom International, https://galcom.org, accessed June 26, 2024.

14. MegaVoice, like GalCom, provides solar-powered audio Bibles that are used widely in CPM ministries. Learn more at https://megavoice.com, accessed June 26, 2024.

15. See The Timothy Initiative, https://ttiglobal.org, accessed June 26, 2024.

16. https://www.sil.org

17. With more than 2,000 translations of this Gospel of Luke video, the JESUS Film is woven into virtually every CPM missionary's strategy.

18. Pioneering Bible translation agency. See more at Seed Company, https://seedcompany.com, accessed June 26, 2024.

19. Faith Comes By Hearing was key to discipling the largely nonliterate Bhojpuri in one of the earliest Church Planting Movements. They have continued to be a part of many subsequent movements. Learn more at https://www.faithcomesbyhearing.com, accessed June 26, 2024.

20. IMB missionaries catalyzing Church Planting Movements in South Asia have attested to collaborative evangelism strategies with EHC in South Asia. See more at Every Home for Christ, https://everyhome.org, accessed July 24, 2024.

21. Building on the pioneering World Christian database developed by David Barrett, Joshua Project maintains what is currently the most visited website for locating unreached people groups, https://joshuaproject.net, accessed June 26, 2024.

22. Gospel portions, testimonies, and Bible recordings in more than 6,000 languages; Global Recordings Network, https://globalrecordings.net/en/, accessed June 26, 2024.

Individual Catalysts

Over the past quarter century several pioneering individuals stand out on the Church Planting Movements landscape. These are men and women who have themselves started Church Planting Movements or coached others to successfully achieve that end.

First on the list would have to be Bill and Susan Smith who were the first Strategy Coordinators appointed by the International Mission Board. A Strategy Coordinator is a missionary to an unreached people group or city with the explicit aim of a Church Planting Movement. Deployed in 1987 to an unreached people group in Asia, Bill Smith went on to train hundreds of missionary Strategy Coordinators, each with the goal of launching a Church Planting Movement.[23]

Two of Smith's earliest protégés were Curtis and Debie Sergeant. Curtis, a Baptist missionary kid who grew up in South Korea and Taiwan, and his wife Debie, launched one of the earliest Church Planting Movements in a remote Asian province before joining Bill Smith in training multitudes of missionaries in CPM strategy formation. In the early 2000s, Sergeant would pioneer the idea of training Christians globally in movements methods. His online CPM training course, *Zúme,* has been translated into fifty-six languages, with more on the horizon.[24]

David and Jan Watson, two of the most effective missionaries trained by Bill Smith, catalyzed one of the earliest Church Planting Movements among a massive unreached community in

---

23. At the time of this writing, Smith is eighty-one years old and still traveling globally to coach and catalyze Church Planting Movements.

24. Sergeant's Zúme training is online at https://zume.training, accessed June 24, 2024. Zúme is the New Testament (koine) Greek word meaning "yeast" and reflects the Matthew 13:33 saying of Jesus: "The kingdom of heaven is like yeast that a woman took and mixed into about sixty pounds of flour until it worked all through the dough."

South Asia. Watson and his son Paul have coached numerous missionaries around the world in using Discovery Bible Studies (DBS) to produce thousands of churches among unreached people groups. In addition to his global training itinerations, Watson has produced online training and is the author of *Contagious Disciple Making*, a book that continues to expand his movement influence.[25]

One of the most productive missionary couples from the Smith and Sergeant school of Strategy Coordinator training was Ying and Grace Kai. Ying, a Taiwanese-American Baptist pastor's son, developed the Training for Trainers (T4T) initiative that has led to numerous fruitful Church Planting Movement endeavors worldwide. In less than a decade the Kais saw more than 1.7 million persons baptized and 150,000 churches started.[26] The Kais inspired two significant books on Training for Trainers that were translated into more than 25 languages.

By the early 2000s Steve and Laura Smith were using the Kais' Training for Trainers to launch a rapidly growing movement among a nonliterate people group in Asia.[27] Steve Smith went on to succeed Curtis Sergeant in teaming up with Bill Smith to train numerous Strategy Coordinator movement catalysts. Smith's impact grew as he worked with e3 Partners, East West Ministries, and BEYOND, before joining with others to launch a new global initiative called 24:14. This international network,

---

25. See David Watson and Paul Watson, *Contagious Disciple Making* (Nashville: Thomas Nelson, 2014) and their website https://www.contagiousdisciplemaking.com, accessed June 24, 2024.

26. See the Kais' profile on the International Mission Board website, https://www.imb.org/175/missionary-profiles/ying-grace-kai/?returnto=ying-and-grace-kai&pageid=127438, accessed June 24, 2024. Ying collaborated with Steve Smith on the widely translated book *T4T: A Discipleship Re-Revolution* (Monument, CO: WIGTake Resources, 2011) and *Ying and Grace Kai's Ying and Grace Kai's Training for Trainers* (Monument, CO: WIGTake Resources, 2018).

27. Steve Smith with Ying Kai, *T4T: A Discipleship Re-Revolution* (Monument, CO: WIGTake Resources, 2011).

inspired by Jesus's words in Matthew 24:14, is an interdenominational collaborative of movement leaders focused on multiplying CPMs among the world's least-reached people groups.[28] Though Steve Smith passed away in 2019, his 24:14 Network continues its mission.

Following Steve Smith's passing, Stan Parks and his wife Kay, missionaries with BEYOND, continued the facilitation of the 24:14 Network, collaborating with movement leaders working among the unreached across the 10/40 Window.[29] Stan's brother, Kent Parks, is the president of BEYOND, a Texas-based mission organization that focuses on "launch[ing] apostolic teams to equip everyday men, women, and children to disciple their own people directly, quickly and exponentially."[30] Keith Parks, the father of Stan and Kent, was president of the Southern Baptist Foreign Mission Board (1980–92) during which time he redirected the agency toward unreached people groups and witnessed the first Church Planting Movements.

I, personally, had the opportunity to serve as a bridge between the pioneering research of Dr. David Barrett and the emergence of Church Planting Movements through Bill Smith, Curtis Sergeant, and others. Barrett, the founding editor of the *World Christian Encyclopedia*,[31] was instrumental in drawing the world's attention to unreached peoples, a priority target for fulfilling the Great Commission. I was Barrett's research associate at the Southern Baptist International Mission Board (1987–88), and

---

28. See the 24:14 website, https://2414now.net, accessed June 24, 2024.

29. The "10/40 Window" is a term coined by Partners International CEO Luis Bush in 1990 to refer to those regions of the eastern hemisphere, located between 10 and *40 degrees north* of the equator, which is home to the vast majority of the world's least-reached people groups.

30. Previously called "Mission to Unreached Peoples," see Beyond's website, "Our Mission," https://beyond.org/about, accessed June 24, 2024.

31. David B. Barrett, ed., *World Christian Encyclopedia* (Oxford: Oxford University Press, 1982).

later directed the agency's Nonresidential Missionary Program, which evolved into Strategy Coordinators. Two of my books, *The Nonresidential Missionary*[32] and *Church Planting Movements*, contributed to the development of the contemporary movement missiology phenomenon.[33]

IMB missionaries Bruce and Gloria Carlton catalyzed their first Church Planting Movement in Cambodia before relocating to South Asia. There, Bruce trained thousands of indigenous missionaries in the Strategy Coordinator methodology for pursuing Church Planting Movements. He subsequently trained scores of IMB missionaries in South Asia to the same end.

The most prolific writer on Church Planting Movements is Steve Addison, an Australian church-planting practitioner and catalyst. Addison's website, Movements.net,[34] has been the Internet platform from which he has promoted numerous influential books, including *Movements that Change the World* (2011), *What Jesus Started* (2012), *Pioneering Movements* (2015), *The Rise and Fall of Movements* (2019), *Your Part in God's Story* (2021), and *Acts and the Movement of God* (2023).

Kevin Greeson and his wife Holley were IMB missionaries to Muslims in Southeast Asia when they entered Smith and Sergeant's Strategy Coordinator training in 1997. Greeson saw one of the largest movements of Muslims to Christ to date. His book *The Camel: How Muslims Are Coming to Faith in Christ*[35]

---

32. David Garrison, *The Non-Residential Missionary* (Monrovia, CA: MARC, 1990).

33. In addition to my 1999 booklet by the same name, I authored the more extensive *Church Planting Movements: How God is Redeeming a Lost World* (Midlothian, VA: WIGTake Resources, 2004).

34. See Addison's website, Movements, https://www.movements.net, accessed June 24, 2024.

35. Kevin Greeson, *The Camel: How Muslims Are Coming to Faith in Christ* (Midlothian, VA: WIGTake Resources, 2010). See also Greeson's new book, *Sowing with Intent: Jesus's Galilean Harvest Movement as a Model for Missions* (Pittsburgh: Dorrance Publishing, 2025).

disclosed the ways that Muslims were being bridged from the Qur'an to the gospel. Greeson continues to coach missionaries worldwide through the US-based ministry Global Gates.[36]

Eric Watt and his wife Becky, the daughter of medical missionaries in India, were among the first Strategy Coordinators trained in 1987. A Yale-educated Assemblies of God missionary, Watt leads RUN (Reaching Unreached Nations) Ministries,[37] collaborating with a network of movement catalysts working among unreached people groups.

Countless other individuals have played prominent roles in the unfolding of Church Planting Movements throughout the world.[38] Among them are Doug Lucas, chief executive officer of Team Expansion and author of *More Disciples*;[39] Warrick Farah, whose *Motus Dei*[40] elevated Church Planting Movements to academic scrutiny; Cynthia (Cindy) Anderson of YWAM who wrote *The Multiplier's Mindset*; Mike Shipman, whose *Any-3: Anyone, Anywhere, Anytime*[41] revealed Jesus's five evangelistic steps that Shipman employed to bring more than 100,000 Muslims to faith in Christ; Jerry Trousdale, author of *Miraculous Movements*;[42] Michael Cooper, whose *Ephesiology* book and curriculum have educated many students of Church Planting Movements; Alan

---

36. Global Gates is a ministry founded in New York City but now working in multiple North American cities to reach through diaspora immigrant populations to foster Church Planting Movements. See https://globalgates.info, accessed June 24, 2024.

37. See RUN's website, https://www.runministries.org, accessed June 24, 2024. RUN's vision statement includes, "MULTIPLY movements that impact their world for good."

38. In addition to these listed are Trevor Larsen, Jeff and Angie Sundell, Nathan and Kari Shank, Neill and Margit Mims, Brad and Lenora Beaman, and researchers Wilson Geisler, Todd Johnson, Bert Hickman, and Justin Long.

39. Doug Lucas, *More Disciples* (Monument, CO: WIGTake Resources, 2019).

40. Motus Dei is Latin for "Movements of God." See https://www.motusdei.network, accessed June 26, 2024.

41. Mike Shipman, *Any 3: Anyone, Anywhere, Anytime* (Monument, CO: WIGTake Resources, 2013).

42. Jerry Trousdale, *Miraculous Movements* (Nashville: Thomas Nelson, 2012).

Hirsch, an Australian missiologist whose book *The Forgotten Ways*[43] brought movemental aspirations to a new generation of Western readers; James Nyman's *Stubborn Perseverance*,[44] which novelized the birthing of a Church Planting Movement; Jon Ralls and the growing *Media to Movements*[45] initiative that is using social media to penetrate inaccessible corners of the globe; and Dave Coles, who has collaborated with several non-Western CPM catalysts to publish accounts of their remarkable movements.[46]

Most important are the unheralded movement leaders who are pioneering Church Planting Movements deep within the 10/40 Window. Victor Choudhrie,[47] Aychi and Tsega B.,[48] Younoussa Djao, David Lim, Shodankeh Johnson, Lipok, Steve and Robin, Sanjay and John, Victor John,[49] and Aila Tasse[50] are each unsung heroes who are catalyzing Church Planting Movements in some of the world's remotest corners.

---

43. Alan Hirsch, *The Forgotten Ways: Reactivating Apostolic Movements* (Ada, MI: Brazos Press, 2016).

44. James Nyman, *Stubborn Perseverance* (Mount Vernon, WA: Mission Network, 2017).

45. See Media to Movements, https://mediatomovements.com, accessed June 26, 2024.

46. See a collection of Dave Coles' books on his website, https://davecoles.freemin.org, accessed April 16, 2025.

47. Victor Choudhrie, MD is sometimes referred to as the father of Church Planting Movements in South Asia. His book *Greet the Church in Your House* (n.p.: Power through Love, 2012) represents only a small part of his decades-long history of mentoring, coaching, and inspiring Church Planting Movements in South Asia and around the world.

48. Aychi B. and Dave Coles, *Living Fire: Advancing God's Kingdom in Challenging Places* (Plano, TX: Beyond, 2025).

49. Victor John (with Dave Coles) has written about an enormous South Asian movement that has catalyzed numerous other movements in his book *Bhojpuri Breakthrough: A Movement that Keeps Multiplying* (Monument, CO: WIGTake Resources, 2019).

50. Aila Tasse leads a sprawling network of movements spanning many countries in East and South Africa. With Dave Coles, Tasse has written his story in *Cabbages in the Desert: How God Transformed a Devout Muslim and Catalyzed Disciple Making Movements Among Unreached Peoples* (Plano, TX: Beyond, 2024).

Jim Slack

Before we conclude this chapter we must acknowledge Dr. Jim Slack, a pioneer in the assessment of movements.[51] CPM assessments trace their origins to Slack, a veteran missionary and researcher who served as the church growth consultant in the IMB's Global Research Department. He was tasked with developing the first Church Planting Movement assessments. Slack's understanding of healthy church was rooted in his Southern Baptist identity and ecclesiology, which influenced his approach to evaluating movements. Slack was suspicious though not dismissive of Pentecostal patterns, particularly *glossolalia* or speaking in tongues, and non-congregational church polity such as the insistence upon ordained clergy for conducting baptism and Communion.

Prior to joining the home office staff of the Southern Baptist mission board, Slack worked as a researcher with the Billy Graham Evangelistic Association, helping lay the foundations of what would become the Lausanne Movement for World Evangelization.[52]

Slack's twenty-five years as a missionary in the Philippines allowed him to refine his research methodologies before applying them throughout the South Asia and Pacific region. His early

---

51. Jim Slack (1938–2018) earned a doctor of ministry degree focusing on orality and literacy from Southwestern Baptist Theological Seminary, where he had also earned his master of divinity degree. He did advanced studies in city mapping and the sociological dynamics in urban environments at the University of Southern Mississippi in Hattiesburg and literature and educational pedagogy at Centenary College in Shreveport, Louisiana. Slack served as president of Southern Baptist Research Fellowship and the International Society for Frontiers Missiology and was a member of both the Evangelical Theological Society and the Evangelical Missiological Society.

52. Art Toalston, "Jim Slack's 'Hello World!' now heard in eternity," International Mission Board, November 19, 2018, https://www.imb.org/2018/11/19/jim-slack/, accessed June 30, 2024.

forays into the more restricted countries that were exhibiting Church Planting Movements revealed some of the difficulties in asking so many questions in a hostile context. To his credit, Slack's methodologies adapted to this new field of inquiry as he sharpened his focus on the most critical questions centered around the quality and quantity of the movements he would examine.

In the chapters that follow, Jim Slack's name will occur often. He was the first among many who were not satisfied with receiving remarkable movement reports. These inquisitive investigators wanted to see for themselves.

In the pages that follow, you will see what Jim Slack and numerous other inquisitive Christians discovered as they explored Church Planting Movements on-site and in depth.

PART TWO

MOVEMENTS AND THEIR ASSESSMENTS

FIVE

THE FIRST CHURCH PLANTING MOVEMENTS

The first reports of Church Planting Movements reached the home office of the International Mission Board in late 1998 and early 1999. The five chapters in this section are drawn from these field reports and the assessments that followed. The assessment reports contained hundreds of pages of both confidential and executive summaries. Rather than document each page within those reports, we will simply note here that all excerpts below are taken directly from those documents.[1]

The Bhojpuri Movement

The Bhojpuri are not a single ethnolinguistic group but rather a sprawling language family of nearly fifty million native speakers

---

1. All statistical information and quotations are taken verbatim from the unpublished, archived reports of the IMB's assessment teams. All information drawn from non-IMB sources is documented where referenced.

stretched across north India and southern Nepal. Within the Bhojpuri language are multiple castes and subgroups (urban, rural, literate, nonliterate). The majority of the Bhojpuri are found in the agricultural villages of Uttar Pradesh and Bihar states. While most of the Bhojpuri are Hindu, they hold a sizable Muslim population as well.

Christian ministry among the Bhojpuri traces back to William Carey's (1793–1834) work in the early nineteenth century. Due to endemic poverty, disease, majority religion opposition, and interethnic militant clashes, the Bhojpuri-speaking region has earned its designation as "the graveyard of missions."[2]

IMB veteran missionaries David and Jan Watson began their Bhojpuri assignment in 1989 with Bill Smith's Strategy Coordinator training. Following a year of language acquisition and cultural adjustment, the Watsons began their work. By 1992 the Watsons were reporting twenty-four Bhojpuri churches with 1,389 church members. Of these, nine were new church starts with seventy-four newly baptized believers over the previous year.

Though some missionaries might be content with nine church starts and seventy-four baptisms in a single year, the Watsons' goal was much higher. David Watson's Strategy Coordinator paradigm asked a big question: What's it going to take for all of the Bhojpuri to come to Christ? His goal was nothing less than the entire fifty million Bhojpuri coming to faith. Watson's ambitious end vision was almost derailed before it began as six of his partner evangelists were murdered early in the ministry.[3]

A breakthrough occurred when the Watsons began to implement what they saw as Jesus's methods for pioneering new work depicted in Luke 10. Watson began sending evangelists two by

---

2. See "June 26 – Pray for India," Operation World, https://operationworld.org/prayer-calendar/06-26/, accessed April 20, 2025.

3. See my book *Church Planting Movements: How God Is Redeeming a Lost World* (Midlothian, VA: WIGTake Resources, 2004), 44.

The First Church Planting Movements

two into Bhojpuri villages to find local "persons of peace." This approach quickly indigenized the work and led to a much more congenial gospel response from the Bhojpuri. As they embraced both the gospel and the church-planter training that Watson offered, the newly-identified Bhojpuri persons of peace became agents of a movement that generated thousands of new disciples and churches within their villages.

Five years later the Watsons were reporting 800 new churches with approximately 50,000 baptized believers meeting regularly for Bible study and worship. By 1997 Watson could only estimate that 10,000 groups were meeting, of which perhaps 2,600 could be designated as organized churches. That same year, Watson estimated 16,000 new believers had been baptized.

By 1999 the Watsons were reporting tens of thousands of new converts, baptized believers, and new church starts. His estimates of as many as 50,000 baptized believers were met initially with incredulity by Watson's own Baptist missionary community, prompting the first CPM assessment the following year.

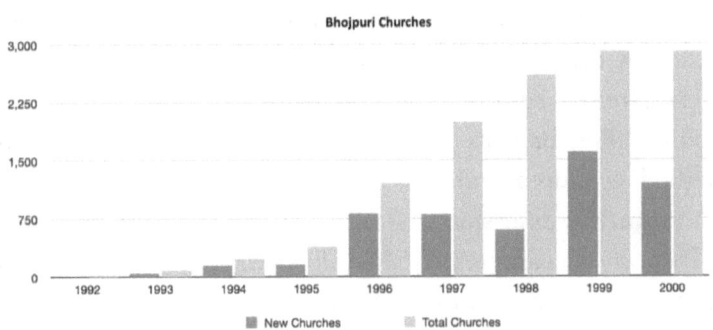

The Bhojpuri Movement Assessment

In October 2000 the first IMB assessment team arrived in north India. The team consisted of Dr. Jim Slack, Dr. Scott Holste

43

(director of the IMB's Global Research Department and veteran missionary from Indonesia and Egypt), and veteran South Asia IMB media missionary James O. Terry. The team was assisted by David Watson and his South Asian partner, Victor John.

Given the broad spread of the movement across two states and two countries, the team concluded the best way to get a good sampling of informants was to attend the annual conference of Bhojpuri Christian leaders. The conference had grown apace with the movement. In 1995, 150 Bhojpuri leaders attended the gathering, a number that grew to more than 1,500 in the year 2000. The assessment team determined that the annual Bhojpuri Leadership Conference had a valid list of 1,600 Bhojpuri pastors, evangelists, and church planters who had attended the conference over the preceding five years.

The team gathered registration information from 525 Bhojpuri leaders attending the 2000 conference. They also conducted what they termed in-depth interviews with individuals and small groups each morning and evening of the conference. In addition to Bhojpuri informants, the team interviewed missionaries from other organizations working among the Bhojpuri including: Mission India, Evangelical Church of India, YWAM, Every Home Crusade, Dutch Reformed Church, Pentecostal Holiness, Free Baptists (Swedish Baptists), Campus Crusade, the Methodist Church, and New Life Fellowship.

From the assessment team's twenty-one-page confidential report, we can identify the information gathered from the informants: when their church was formed; how many members; how many churches their church started over the past year; church attendance numbers; baptisms over the past year; new works started compared to the previous year; size of the leadership conference and its growth by year; worship practices (preaching and worship songs in the Bhojpuri language); issues encountered such as the existence of *glossolalia* (speaking

The First Church Planting Movements

in tongues), exorcisms, and healings; church polity (how the churches were organized and how worship services were conducted); theology; soteriology (doctrine of salvation); and leadership training.

Regarding leadership training, the team reported that leadership training has

> from the beginning, (been) a major concern and activity of the Bhojpuri leadership. There are four very common training approaches that exist among the Bhojpuri. In the order of their importance, frequency, and volume of participation they are: a) the weekly mentoring of the Man of Peace by the church planter who has led him to the Lord and is mentoring him to be both a pastor and a church planter; b) the eight Consortium training centers, c) the newly emerging training programs of the various agencies who have come to assist in the evangelization of the Bhojpuri, and d) the occasional LEAD [the name given to the IMB itinerant training missionaries] training courses that have been offered over at least ten years, mainly to the more established Swedish Baptist pastors and leaders.

In addition to their conference interviews, the team created an extensive contextual history of the Bhojpuri work dating back more than a century. The team identified 40–80 Protestant churches (primarily Baptist, Methodist, and Anglican) among the Bhojpuri-speaking people. This background information lent context to the nine years of annual statistical reports provided by the Watsons.

The assessment team acknowledged that the size of the movement, which they concluded to be in the hundreds of thousands of new believers, was too large for them to obtain a true random sampling, and this led the team to make cautious conclusions regarding the movement's size. In their confidential report the team used what they called a conservative "reduction formula." They described this formula as follows:

> ... assuming that the churches in (the) whole movement performed at a level less than the averages of those attending the Conference. One-half of the churches were calculated at the observed averages; while one-fourth were calculated at 75% of the averages, with the remaining one-fourth calculated at 50% of the averages.

Based upon the team's interviews, the Watsons' annual statistical report, and the corroboration by Watson's network of evangelical partners, Slack's "reduction formula" estimated the movement's size. They presented these estimates as low, medium, and high:

> Low estimate: 3,277 total churches with 224,722 members and 49,636 baptisms the previous year.

> Medium estimate: 4,369 total churches with 299,629 total members and 66,181 baptisms the previous year.

> High estimate: 5,461 total churches with 374,536 total members and 82,727 baptisms the previous year.

In an aside to the author, Slack confided, "If I had to bet, I would guess that the high estimate is the most accurate."[4]

The team's methodology had to be adapted to give birth to a new type of assessment. No longer did they have the luxury of gathering data as openly as Dr. Slack had done in the Philippines. Nonetheless, they had confirmed one of the earliest Church

---

4. Conversation between Slack and the author in Winter 2000.

Planting Movements on record, and their assessment methods would improve.[5]

A Bangladeshi Muslim Movement

Even before engaging the Bhojpuri, the English Baptist cobbler William Carey came face-to-face with the twenty to thirty million Bengali people of South Asia. Soon after establishing his base in the Bengal city of Serampore in 1794, Carey determined that any successful missionary work among Bengalis would require a Bible in their native language, a task he spent the next six years accomplishing.

At the beginning of his work, Carey faced a critical choice. There were two sizable communities of Bengali speakers, Hindus and Muslims, with very different worldviews. While the Hindu and Muslim communities held much of the Bengali language in common, their conversations varied radically when they turned to spiritual and religious matters. The religious terms used by Hindu Bengalis were steeped in ancient Sanskrit, while Bengali Muslims used words that had their roots in Arabic and Urdu.

Perhaps anticipating a more responsive hearing from the Hindus and Tribals, Carey adapted his biblical vocabulary from the Sanskrit language. It proved to be a choice that would shape not only his New Testament translation but the destiny of the Bengali people for the next two centuries. Carey could not have

---

5. In 2007 a further survey of the Bhojpuri work was attempted by others, but without IMB involvement. This book has not been informed by these subsequent assessments beyond what is reported above. In the years that followed the IMB's assessment, this graveyard of missions became a major Christian harvest field. Numerous agencies and individuals (using a variety of church-planting methods) proliferated, and the multiplication of churches spread into numerous other unreached people groups in the region. For firsthand insight into the work among the Bhojpuri and other neighboring people groups, see Victor John's *Bhojpuri Breakthrough: A Movement that Keeps Multiplying* (Monument, CO: WIGTake Resources, 2019).

imagined that by the end of the twentieth century Islam would vastly eclipse the Hindu and Tribal Bengali populations, swelling to more than 150 million Muslims. For these Muslim Bengalis, the Carey translation—with its Sanskrit vocabulary—appeared to be a Hindu or even pagan book. Not until the 1980s would a Muslim-idiom translation, the *Kitabul Mukkadas* (literally, *the Holy Book*) appear, giving Bengali Muslims their first intelligible glimpse into the gospel message.

In July 1997, following decades of work among Bengali Hindus and Tribals, Southern Baptists transferred missionaries Kevin and Holley Greeson to the majority Muslim population. The Greesons hoped to see a fruitful response from Muslims as well. Already fluent in Bengali, the Greesons began their new assignment with Bill Smith's Strategy Coordinator training.

In their first report submitted in 1998 the Greesons indicated no churches or baptisms among Bengali Muslims. Soon afterward, however, Greeson came upon a network of thousands of indigenously-led, Muslim-background converts to the Christian faith. As he explored the reasons for these Muslim conversions, Greeson learned that new Muslim-background believers were using Qur'anic passages that referenced Jesus to bridge a conversation from the Qur'an to the gospel. As the Greesons and their partners adopted a similar approach, they too found receptivity.[6]

By 2001 Greeson was reporting seventy-nine new church starts with 2,300 baptized Muslim-background members. When coupled with the indigenous movement, he estimated that tens of thousands of Muslims across the country had come to faith in Christ. Realizing that such numbers from a Muslim mission field were unprecedented, Greeson reached out to his regional leadership and the Global Research Department for an assessment.

---

6. The Qur'anic bridges used in this ministry were published in Kevin Greeson's *The Camel, How Muslims Are Coming to Faith in Christ* (Midlothian, VA: WIGTake Resources, 2007).

The First Church Planting Movements

That same year the IMB's Global Research Department began their preparatory work for an onsite survey.

The First Bengali Muslim Movement Assessment

In compiling his background research, the IMB's Jim Slack drew from a number of sources. These included published demographic data, reports by Bengali Baptist churches, letters from a Japanese-American who had spent many years mentoring the leader of the indigenous Bengali movement, and two separate field surveys of the work conducted in the early 1990s. One of those surveys was led by Dr. Cal Guy, mission professor at Southwestern Baptist Theological Seminary. The other had been funded by the Pew Charitable Trust with assistance from the U.S. Center for World Mission in Pasadena, California. These sources provided Slack with ample material for crafting an extensive profile of the Bengali context before arriving on site.

In May and June 2002, Slack led an IMB assessment team to Bangladesh. The team consisted of Dr. Jim Haney, the new director of the Global Research Department and veteran West Africa missionary, along with Dr. Randy Rains, a former missionary to Bangladesh and fluent Bengali speaker. From the Asian side, Greeson recruited a cadre of local translators and drivers.

The assessment team segregated their survey into two parts: one focused on the IMB-led church starts and the other was directed toward the larger indigenous movement. According to their published report, the team sought to interview randomly-selected informants with an eye toward capturing testimony from a spectrum of church leaders, lay members, women, and both nonliterate and literate informants.

From the IMB-led movement the team gathered 67 randomly selected interviews from each of the twenty-one districts in which the IMB had evangelistic outreach. They determined that the IMB-led movement had grown from 123 Muslim-background believers (MBBs) in 1995 to 4,138 MBBs in 2002. The typical church the team surveyed was less than four years old, had thirty members, and had baptized eight new believers the previous year. Their survey revealed that these churches had averaged starting 3.3 new churches the preceding year. This same movement had seen 163 baptisms each month in 2001. In the first six months of 2002 the IMB-led movement had seen 455 baptisms per month and had grown faster than Greeson had indicated in his annual report.

The assessment team then turned their attention to the larger, indigenously-led movement. The team was able to conduct eighty-three randomly selected interviews. From these interviews the team concluded that the larger movement had evangelists from a Muslim background working in twenty-nine of the nation's sixty-four districts. They were able to interview informants from seventeen of these districts. In the seventeen districts the team confirmed the existence of 160 evangelists ministering in them. These evangelists were starting new churches and/or serving as pastors of small, local gatherings. The team concluded that the seventeen districts had a total of 1,186 pastors with 2,329 churches that were home to approximately 52,357 members. They further determined that in 2001 this larger, indigenously-led work had seen 9,651 baptisms across the seventeen districts.

From this base of interviews in seventeen districts, the team couldn't resist making a projection of how large the movement might be if it were, as reported, present throughout the country. From that projection across the whole of the twenty-nine districts, they estimated there was likely a total of 357 district evangelists, with roughly 2,293 pastors, serving in and among 3,973 churches with approximately 89,315 members. The team further projected it was reasonable to estimate more than 23,000 new baptisms had taken place across the nation in the year 2001.

The First Church Planting Movements

If the assessment team's projection was accurate, it was possible there was a total of 89,315 baptized believers in the larger movement. When coupled with the IMB missionaries' 4,138 baptized believers, the total number of Muslim-background converts across Bangladesh could be as high as 93,453 baptized believers.

In addition to assessing the size of each movement, the team explored the spiritual health of the churches and believers. The team leader correlated numerous demographic (vocation, age, education, religious background, etc.), theological (what do you believe about Jesus, the Bible, Muhammad, the Qur'an, etc.), ecclesiological, and missiological issues. The total number of informants interviewed in both streams was 150 of whom, unfortunately, only 10 were women. The reason given for this paucity of female informants was the local sensitivities regarding outsiders talking with women.

The team further explored: (1) the degree of involvement in religion of each informant prior to conversion; (2) knowledge of apostasy within the movement; (3) degree of syncretism within the movement; (4) locations of church meetings and whether the meetings were open or secret; (5) the nature and extent of the informant's education; (6) the nature and extent of discipleship within the movement; (7) whether and to what degree the informants had received outside financial assistance; and (8) whether and to what extent the converts had been persecuted.

Despite the team's efforts to keep a low profile, their probes sometimes resulted in public melees. The assessment team described the beating of local informants with some church leaders temporarily jailed. Afterwards, the team stated that these harassed believers remained bold in their testimonies.

The assessment team's qualitative findings were insightful. When asked whether some believers had returned to Islam, 91.7 percent of informants said no; 8.3 percent said yes; and 1.97 percent said they didn't know. When asked if new believers still mixed some of their Islamic practices with their Christian practices, 22 percent said yes, while 77 percent said no. When asked if the informants received outside personal or financial assistance, 15 percent said yes; 8.75 percent said rarely; 61.25 percent said no; and 12 percent said they didn't know.

A warning sign appeared in the report as each of the district evangelists were regarded as missionaries and thus received "a type of salary and a given amount to establish them in business." Establishing a business provided the evangelists with a base of operations and a means of support that prevented the need for foreign subsidies.

In its conclusion the assessment confirmed the existence of two vibrant movements taking place in Bangladesh. The older and larger work had been catalyzed by a local, Muslim-background believer. The younger movement, the one that Greeson had reported, was smaller yet growing rapidly.

In February 2003 the team issued a ninety-page confidential report of their assessment. In addition to their findings, the team generated several pages of recommendations and concerns aimed at strengthening both works. In their report the assessment team confirmed that thousands of Muslims in Bangladesh were coming to faith and baptism, accompanied by numerous new church starts.

A Cambodian Movement

By the end of the twentieth century, Southeast Asia was still reeling from the turbulent events of the preceding decades. The Vietnam War (1955–75) and the devastation wreaked by the Pol Pot Khmer Rouge regime in Cambodia (1975–78) had left deep scars on the Buddhist inhabitants of the region. Out of this context, extraordinary reports of new believers and churches began to appear in the late 1990s continuing into the twenty-first century.

The turmoil of the 1970s had left Cambodia in ruins. The atheistic Khmer Rouge were particularly cruel to the country's 6,000,000 Buddhists and the fledgling population of 23,000 Christians.[7] When Pol Pot's regime ended in 1978, some 21 to 24 percent of the nation's population, 1.5–2 million citizens, had been massacred by the Khmer Rouge.[8]

Baptist work in the country began in 1993, when the IMB's Cooperative Services International Department (the division responsible for work in closed countries) assigned Bruce and Gloria Carlton, an experienced church-planting couple, as missionary Strategy Coordinators to this new field.

Carlton had read the booklet *Church Planting Movements* and received some cursory training in the Strategy Coordinator paradigm by this author and fellow missionary Scott Holste before commencing his work. Soon after, Carlton launched what he called the Rural Leadership Training Program (RLTP) to stimulate new church starts throughout Cambodia.

By the end of 1993 Carlton and his Cambodian partners had planted fourteen new churches in five of the nation's twenty-one provinces. In 1994 the total number of churches grew to forty-two in ten provinces. During this time Christian and Missionary Alliance churches, which had begun Cambodian work in 1923, were also seeing unprecedented growth. By the end of 1994 evangelical churches were meeting in each of the country's twenty-one provinces.

When the Baptist Convention of Cambodia held its annual

---

7. David Barrett, George Kurian, and Todd Johnson, eds., *World Christian Encyclopedia*, Vol. 1, 163.

8. Wikipedia, "Pol Pot," https://en.wikipedia.org/wiki/Pol_Pot, last modified May 21, 2025. For more extensive information see Ben Kiernan, *The Pol Pot Regime: Race, Power, and Genocide in Cambodia under the Khmer Rouge, 1975-79* (New Haven, CT: Yale University Press, 2008).

meeting in 1996, Carlton's team reported seventy affiliated churches had been planted by participants in his Rural Leadership Training Program initiatives. By the end of 1997 there were 120 or more Baptist churches. Carlton was now convinced that the work he had begun would continue under the indigenous leadership left behind. That same year the Carltons transferred to India with its limitless opportunities to pioneer new movements among the nation's millions of unreached peoples.

Following the Carltons' departure the IMB continued to appoint new Baptist missionaries to Cambodia. Some of these missionaries were movement catalysts, while others—though exceptional in many ways—were not advocates of movements. In the late 1990s Baptist missions in Cambodia began eliminating subsidies for training events such as the RLTP that had been vital to the movement's advance. These subsidies had not gone to supporting pastors or church buildings but rather the training and theological education of lay leaders who led the work as bi-vocational church leaders and planters. As these training subsidies evaporated, so too did the Baptist role in the movement.

Cambodian Movement Assessment

In 2000 the IMB's regional leader for Southeast Asia requested an assessment of the Cambodian work. In 2001 Jim Slack began compiling a profile of the country and its people before conducting an onsite survey. The preliminary research gathered the political, religious, demographic, and missionary history of the country.

In August 2001 Slack recruited veteran East Africa missionary Dr. Jim Maroney to join him in the assessment. With friendly cooperation from the Cambodian Baptist Convention, the two men ventured into the summer heat of Cambodia and began their onsite survey.

The men determined that only forty-five churches would need to be surveyed to achieve a 20 percent sampling of the movement. The team interviewed seventy-one informants of whom forty-four were pastors and twenty-seven were lay members who had come from a cross-sampling of sixty churches. In the final analysis the team had gathered informants from twenty-eight percent of the 213 churches listed in the Baptist denomination's registry. However, samplings are only as valid as the universe (the total size of the population) from which they are taken. In the case of the Cambodian assessment, the team's universe was too small.

The assessment team concluded there was no Church Planting Movement in Cambodia. However, the assessment team was wrong; the Cambodian movement was actually booming. In fact, the Cambodian Christian population exploded from fewer than 23,000 in 1970 to more than half a million by 2022. So, how did the assessment team miss out on the fastest growing church in Southeast Asia?

The answer appears to be found in the limited scope of the assessment team's investigation. The CPM assessment team restricted their sampling universe to Cambodian Baptist churches. In a sense, though, they were correct. There was no longer a Baptist Church Planting Movement in Cambodia. The Baptist role in the movement had waned in the years after the departure of its catalysts, Bruce and Gloria Carlton.

When the assessment team queried Cambodian Baptist leaders, they reported they were not aware of a Church Planting Movement in their country, even though the number of Baptist churches had grown to 203 in less than a decade. However, subsequent reports from other sources in the country told quite a different story.

One of Carlton's short-term missionary colleagues in

Cambodia was a young man named Steve Hyde. Hyde was a Baptist missionary kid who had grown up in the Philippines, where his father was killed by Islamic terrorists.[9] After college Hyde served for two years in Cambodia under the supervision of Bruce Carlton, where he collaborated in Carlton's CPM strategy. In the early 2000s Hyde married a Cambodian woman and immigrated to the country as an independent missionary. Shortly thereafter, Hyde began his doctoral research on the state of the growing church in his newly adopted homeland.

Hyde's research revealed that the growth of the church in Cambodia had continued to increase exponentially after Carlton's departure, though largely outside of Baptist circles. In 2006 Hyde started what he called "the Antioch Institute" to train pastors, a decentralized model not unlike Carlton's Rural Leadership Training Program. On his website Hyde reported in 2024: "Currently, we teach nearly 4,000 leaders a year through the network of Antioch Institute training centers. They are taught through nearly 200 training centers across Cambodia."[10]

By the summer of 2016, 2,500 evangelical church leaders in Cambodia met in a nationwide Christian conference. Then, in January 2023, *Christianity Today* further confirmed Hyde's report of an ongoing Church Planting Movement. Quoting the *World Christian Database,* the article attested to half a million Christians in the country, almost 3 percent of the nation's 17 million citizens.[11]

---

9. James Yates, "Coworkers Remember Bill Hyde as a Model of Radical Grace," in Baptist Press, March 11, 2003, https://www.baptistpress.com/resource-library/news/coworkers-remember-bill-hyde-as-a-model-of-radical-grace/.

10. Steve and Nuit Hyde, "Antioch Institute," Asia for Jesus, https://www.asiaforjesus.org/ministries/antioch-institute/, accessed July 28, 2024.

11. Kate Shellnut, "Cambodians Usher in a Miraculous Moment for Christianity" in *Christianity Today*, May 19, 2017. Also see, James Thompson, "Born Again and Again: Cambodian Evangelicals Celebrate 100 Years" in *Christianity Today*, January 25, 2023.

The First Church Planting Movements

A broader assessment universe by Slack's survey would have revealed that the evangelical church in Cambodia continued to exhibit massive growth throughout the decades following the Khmer Rouge pogroms. However, as the Baptist denomination in the country moved toward established church buildings with paid pastoral leadership, they abandoned the lay-led house church movement that the Carltons had initiated. Consequently, the rapid growth that began among Baptists in the 1990s had ossified by the time of Slack's survey in 2001 and migrated to other denominational, para-church, and nondenominational expressions.

From its humble beginnings of fewer than 23,000 in 1970, and the subsequent losses suffered under the Pol Pot regime, the evangelical population had grown to more than half a million by 2023. Most of the growth, however, occurred outside the denominational boundaries of the Cambodian Baptists.

With the benefit of hindsight, the Cambodian experience had much to teach. Carlton's CPM missiological methods had spawned a movement, but the movement expired with a return to more traditional church structures and strictures. However, as Carlton's methods were reintroduced by Steve Hyde and others, the movement found fertile soil to continue its remarkable growth.

The error in the assessment team's methodology was in their presumption that this movement was confined to a single denomination; when in fact it was a Jesus movement that cared little for denominational boundaries. While Baptists had been instrumental in the movement's launching, their traditional wineskin had proven unable to contain the burgeoning new wine that flowed unhindered throughout the country.

SIX

COMMUNIST, BERBER, AND TRIBAL MOVEMENTS

The unfolding story of Church Planting Movements and assessments was now moving outside of Asia. What would they find in other places? As reports of movements surfaced in Latin America and North Africa, would these reports mirror those in Asia? Or were these rapidly multiplying churches and disciples unique to the unreached peoples of Asia? Our first stop is Cuba, where a Kingdom movement would confront a Marxist movement.

A Cuban Movement

Baptist missions began in Cuba in the 1880s with a comity agreement dividing the eastern and western regions of the country between American Baptist and Southern Baptist missionaries. Both works grew incrementally over the next century until January 1, 1959 when everything changed. The Communist coup d'état led by Fidel Castro brought major disruptions. In 1966 Castro expelled all remaining missionaries from the country and implemented a campaign of persecution, imprisonment, and even martyrdom against the struggling church.

In the mid-1990s Southern Baptists reengaged Cuba by assigning a nonresidential missionary based outside the country to work with Baptist partners inside the country.[1] Over the next few years, rapid multiplication of new believers and churches began taking place.[2]

Beginning in the latter half of the 1990s, both the eastern and western Baptist denominations reported new growth. In 1995 Baptists in the country reported 654 churches; in 1996—678 churches; in 1997—781 churches; in 1998—975 churches; in 1999—1,549 churches; in 2000—2,387 churches; in 2001—4,020 churches. By February 2002 Cuban Baptists were reporting 5,657 Baptist churches.

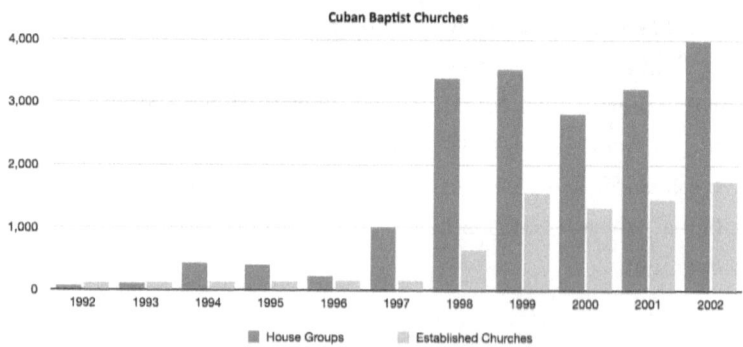

Throughout this period, Cuba's government maintained strict prohibitions against constructing new church buildings.

---

1. For the nonresidential missionary paradigm, see David Garrison, *The Nonresidential Missionary* (Pasadena, CA: MARC, 1990).

2. In 2012 Southern Baptist missionary, Kurt Urbanek, published his doctoral research on the movement in *Cuba's Great Awakening* (pub. by author, 2014).

At the same time, the movement was spreading into hundreds of home-based *casas de oración* (houses of prayer) and *casa cultos* (home worship) gatherings. As late as 1990 the two Baptist conventions had recorded no houses of prayer and no home worship groups. A decade later they were reporting 2,530 such home-based groups. The proliferation of these unofficial meeting places was keeping pace with the growing number of new believers that had risen from 13,358 in 1990 to 183,502 in 2001.

These reports from the late 1990s prompted the International Mission Board to conduct a thorough investigation. Around the year 2000 the IMB's nonresidential missionary to Cuba invited the Global Research Department to assess the work. Preparations began in late 2001.

Cuban Movement Assessment

In early 2002 the IMB's Global Research Department commenced its survey of the work in Cuba. The team preceded its onsite visit with voluminous information regarding the history of the people and the work of multiple denominations to plant churches in the country. Jim Slack led the assessment team, recruiting veteran missionary and Spanish-speaker Dennis Jones, and Spanish-speaking missionaries Dr. Roy and Dirce Cooper.

Despite the government's opposition, the team was able to gather "about 400 verbatim interviews" with full input from 215 informants (68 percent male and 32 percent female). Though the team limited their onsite interviews to members of the Baptist denomination, they also compiled church growth trend lines for Methodists, Episcopalians, Pentecostals, Presbyterians, Seventh Day Adventists, and even Jehovah's Witnesses. Though the information from these other denominations was not gleaned from random samplings, it did help to provide a growth context for comparison with the movements that were taking place among Baptists.

The assessment team examined the Baptist churches in both the eastern and western divisions of the country, and their information gathering was prodigious. The team's report included typical monthly salaries for a dozen different job types in the country, from doctors and engineers to taxi drivers and field workers. They used this information as a basis of comparison with the salaries of local pastors, evangelists, and church planters. The team also documented the costs of forty different staples in the local economy, from clothes to food, to determine the cost of living for church leaders. All of this data was in addition to such elemental church-related questions regarding doctrine, church polity, and the percentages of Christians who owned their own Bibles.

The team carefully documented the nature of the churches' worship and discipleship. Their survey included the different types of leaders and documented how many had seminary training, how many were ordained, and how many were serving as local missionaries or evangelists. The report also described the pastoral education and leadership certification processes.

Given Cuba's long mission history, the team was anxious to identify the turning points that had led to the recent rapid growth. Unexpectedly the team discovered that it was the very pressures exerted by the Communist government that had contributed significantly to the movement. When the government refused permission for new church buildings, the growing numbers of believers were dismissively directed by the government to meet in homes. This led to the proliferation of houses of prayer and home worship.

The assessment team observed that meeting in homes had given rise to lay leadership and removed from the movement's growth the limitations of constructing brick-and-mortar church buildings. The country's isolation from the outside world also insulated the movement from foreign subsidies and the dependency they tended to foster.

Not everything the assessment team found in the Cuba movement was deemed healthy. The Landmarkist ecclesiology that Cuban Baptists inherited from nineteenth- and early twentieth-century missionaries was still influencing the church. The Landmarkist insistence upon limiting baptizing authority to ordained ministers could not keep up with the number of new believers seeking baptism. While baptized church membership had grown from roughly 6,000 in 1989 to 43,829 in 2002, the assessment team found that as many as 179,500 believers were still awaiting baptism from an ordained pastor.

In January 2003 the team issued a sixty-seven-page confidential report and seven-page executive summary of their findings. The team's two reports of more than 34,500 words provided a virtual exegesis of the movement. To assist those engaged in the movement, the team's report offered sixteen specific recommendations for the Church Planting Movements going forward.

When I visited Cuba in 2014, the superintendent of Baptist churches reported that ten thousand churches had been planted over the previous decades. Even the Communist Office of Religious Affairs admitted grudgingly that some 10 percent of the country was now evangelical Christian.

A Muslim Berber Movement

All of the governments of North Africa are hostile to Christian missionary activity, and this particular country was one of the most severe. For this reason we cannot name the specific Berber people group in this report or the name of the country in which they reside.

The Berbers, numbering more than thirty million people across twenty distinct ethnolinguistic groups, are the indigenous inhabitants of North Africa. They predate the Arab and all other immigrations to the region. Historically marginalized by the invasions that plagued their land, many Berbers who resisted assimilation retreated to the mountains and deserts. In addition to their numbers in North Africa, there is also a sizable Berber diaspora in Europe.

Though most Berbers are Muslim, this specific Berber people had resisted efforts by the government to Arabize them, and this contributed to their ambivalence toward the Islamic religion. By 2000, stories were circulating among evangelicals in the West of growing numbers of new believers and churches among this Berber people group.

In 1991 Southern Baptists assigned a veteran missionary couple as Strategy Coordinators to this Berber people. The couple was unable to reside in North Africa, so they took on a nonresidential assignment based in Europe, where they could partner with the millions of diaspora Berbers living there. These diaspora Berbers played a crucial role in fueling the growth of the movement back in their North African homeland.

The Strategy Coordinator contributed to radio broadcasts, JESUS Film production and distribution, and Bible translation in the Berber language. These efforts soon proved effective and fueled an acceleration of new believers and churches in North Africa.

Within a few years the Strategy Coordinator reported scores of identifiable churches in North African cities as well as an unknown number scattered throughout the Berber hinterlands. In 1992 the missionary reported eleven churches; in 1995—eighteen churches; in 2000—forty churches. By 2001 he estimated there were at least fifty churches with as many as 20,000 baptized Muslim-background believers from this Berber people residing in their North African country.

Communist, Berber, and Tribal Movements

These reports from a region long known to be hostile to the gospel prompted the Strategy Coordinator to invite an assessment team to help investigate the nature, strengths, and weaknesses of the work. In 2001 an assessment team began taking shape.

The Berber Movement Assessment

In October 2002 Jim Slack, with assistance from francophone missionary Dr. Robert Shehane, and the IMB's French-speaking nonresidential missionary, led an on-site survey of the Berber movement. The men were assisted with logistics by local Berber Christians who were bilingual in French and the Berber language.

Initial research suggested that many of the Berber Christians in the rural interior related back to urban "mother churches." Consequently, the team focused their interviews in three urban centers. They selected as randomly as possible informants from the leaders and members of the mother churches and those rural believers who could access the central churches for interviews. The team admitted this was not ideal but was the best they could achieve under the circumstances.

The team conducted interviews with two- to three hundred informants and supplemented them with eleven different sources of information. Nonetheless, the team found that "as best [they] could determine, no more than three or four people within [this] Christian movement even knew just how many . . . [Berber] Christian churches there were."

The assessment team faced significant hurdles. In addition to government restrictions, much of the Berber movement was inaccessible as it was scattered across the country's mountainous and bandit-riddled interior. The team's candid report noted:

The surveyors were literally putting the pieces of a church growth presence together like a puzzle on a table. In this case the table was the entire northern coast of [the country] and the mountain range that covered that entire coastal area. In order to put the puzzle together, the surveyors had to carefully glean from every believer they met, the information each one had about any church or churches they knew, and where they were in those mountains.

The assessment report further hinted at the team's frustration with the limitations of their survey as they noted

> in-depth and detailed information about churches that were not interviewed was difficult to secure. And, there was not the opportunity to spend the usual two hours interviewing each person who was available. The surveyors literally caught them on the run as they came and went from these major centers during the time the surveyors were there. As a result, to succeed, the assessment had to include enough individual interviews of a narrative nature, which had as many of the quantitative questions answered as was possible under hurried circumstances in order to determine the scope and nature of the movement.

Despite these challenges the team estimated there were eleven Berber churches in the country in 1993; sixteen churches in 1995; twenty churches in 1997; thirty-five churches in 1999; and fifty-five churches in 2001. By 2002 the team estimated there were least sixty-five formal Berber churches, with more informal house churches meeting in the country's interior.

The team estimated annual baptisms within the Berber churches were around 136 in 1996; 400 in 1998; and more than 400 in the year 2000. In the first nine months of 2002, the Berber

Christians were already numbering between 750 and 800 baptisms. Total church membership was calculated to be about 1,000 in 1997; and 1,600 in 1999, with projections of between 4,000 and 5,000 by January of 2003 when the report was completed.

When exploring the qualitative nature of the movement, the team found that believers represented a wide range of ages, from children to senior adults. Youth ministry and discipleship were strongly advocated in the churches, and evangelistic outreach was common. They observed that women comprised about 30 percent of the church congregations assessed.

The report included a description of leadership training and local church worship and found them to be closely aligned with evangelical norms. Reflecting their Baptist values the team stated:

> First, the churches are clearly evangelical in understanding, worship and practice. Second, they are sound when it comes to Baptist doctrine. When the interviewers went over the evangelism and discipleship materials in two of the three central churches, which is what all of the other churches use, they were very Baptist in doctrinal coverage and content. They were very conservative. Third, a few, clearly a small number, of the modules produced in [one of the cities] in the media ministry had a slight Pentecostal flavor to them, but they were far outweighed by the number of very solid New Testament, evangelical, and Baptist-oriented pieces. Fourth, every radio program site was using Baptist materials, even Trans World Radio programs.

In June 2003 the team issued a 43-page confidential report and 12-page executive summary of their findings. Despite the limitations of their onsite access, the team's final report included centuries of contextual church history in the country, profiles of multidenominational outreach to the Berber group, 10 years of reported growth statistics for membership and churches, and, of course, data gleaned from their onsite informants. The team also examined the role of Christian radio broadcasts into the interior, and the nature of new church starts emerging out of central "mother churches," as well as the role of the diaspora ministries in fueling the movement.

The team concluded that the Berber work appeared to be an emerging Church Planting Movement, but with some reservations. While the churches they visited were vibrant and growing, their members worshipped in traditional church buildings with recognized pastoral leaders. Though the team did not personally witness the sort of multiplying house churches that were the hallmark of other movements, informants indicated the urban churches were also hiving off members to form new groups in rural areas where church buildings were less common.

An Adivasi Movement

The term *Adivasi* is the collective name the Indian government has given to various ethnolinguistic tribal peoples scattered across the subcontinent. Due to intense anti-Christian persecution from the Hindu nationalist majority in this state, we will refrain from disclosing the name of the state or the specific people group name. Instead we will refer to them as simply, the Adivasi.

With a population of about 850,000, the Adivasi comprised 2.5 percent of this Indian state's total population. The government labeled them Adivasi (primitive) because they followed a variety of local deities rather than the majority religions of Hinduism and Islam. The Adivasi were primarily agriculturalists, practicing a mixture of animistic and Hindu beliefs.

British Baptists began missionary work in this Indian state in

1822. The work proved difficult, with one or two churches planted each year for the next century and a half. In 1972, responding to the growing ecumenism among Protestants, Baptists in the state withdrew from the larger ecumenical denomination to form their own Baptist Evangelical denomination.

In the early 1990s Southern Baptists began exploring opportunities for ministry and witness among the Adivasi. In 1995 Calvin and Margaret Fox, agricultural missionaries with twenty-seven years of experience in the Philippines, were transferred to work among the Adivasi. The Foxes brought with them fruitful evangelistic and agricultural strategies that had been developed by the Asian Rural Life and Development Center in the Philippines. Foremost among these was Sloping Agricultural Land Technology (SALT), which taught rural farmers how to cultivate crops on hillsides, greatly increasing their productivity.

In 1997 J. O. Terry, the IMB's regional media consultant, launched a radio program called "School in the Air," which featured Bible storying sets in the Adivasi language. The potent addition of chronological Bible storying to Fox's agricultural ministries soon began to stimulate a marked increase in new believers, churches, and outreach groups. These outreach groups were composed of small gatherings of listeners to the Bible story radio broadcasts.

Local Indian partners were critical to the work's advance. Dr. S. P., a forestry professor at the university in the state's capital city, was a visionary leader and helped to establish eight hundred evangelistic agro-forestry societies across the state. Within a few years, the Foxes were reporting thousands of new believers among the Adivasi with a commensurate number of new churches.[3]

---

3. Erich Bridges, "Missionary Calvin Fox dies: helped end 'hunger season' for millions of Asians," in *Baptist Press*, December 18, 2003, https://www.baptistpress.com/resource-library/news/missionary-calvin-fox-dies-helped-end-hunger-season-for-millions-of-asians/.

When the Foxes began their work in 1995, there were 194 Baptist churches in the state with 10,030 members. History does not record how many of these churches were composed of Adivasi. Over the next eight years Fox would only report having personally helped to start seventy-five new Adivasi churches in 1999, a number that would grow to 232 churches by 2003. By the late 1990s, though, the Adivasi were starting new churches on their own. Fox estimated that the total number of Adivasi churches had grown from 1,215 in 1999 to 2,249 in 2023. The rapid and indigenous growth among the Adivasi prompted the IMB's area director to invite the Global Research Department in 2002 to conduct an assessment.

As the assessment was underway, Calvin Fox, who was on stateside assignment in the U.S., suffered a heart attack and passed away. In his eulogy of Fox, IMB executive vice president Clyde Meador said, "He led in outreach efforts that saw 100 churches become more than 2,000 churches in these last few years."[4]

Fox's passing ended the IMB's direct involvement with the Adivasi movement, but its indigenous growth continued well into the twenty-first century under the leadership of Dr. S. P. and the emerging Adivasi-led churches.

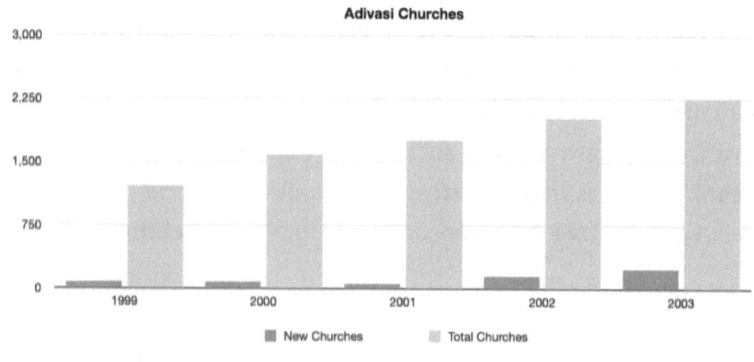

4. Bridges, "Missionary Calvin Fox dies."

Communist, Berber, and Tribal Movements

1822. The work proved difficult, with one or two churches planted each year for the next century and a half. In 1972, responding to the growing ecumenism among Protestants, Baptists in the state withdrew from the larger ecumenical denomination to form their own Baptist Evangelical denomination.

In the early 1990s Southern Baptists began exploring opportunities for ministry and witness among the Adivasi. In 1995 Calvin and Margaret Fox, agricultural missionaries with twenty-seven years of experience in the Philippines, were transferred to work among the Adivasi. The Foxes brought with them fruitful evangelistic and agricultural strategies that had been developed by the Asian Rural Life and Development Center in the Philippines. Foremost among these was Sloping Agricultural Land Technology (SALT), which taught rural farmers how to cultivate crops on hillsides, greatly increasing their productivity.

In 1997 J. O. Terry, the IMB's regional media consultant, launched a radio program called "School in the Air," which featured Bible storying sets in the Adivasi language. The potent addition of chronological Bible storying to Fox's agricultural ministries soon began to stimulate a marked increase in new believers, churches, and outreach groups. These outreach groups were composed of small gatherings of listeners to the Bible story radio broadcasts.

Local Indian partners were critical to the work's advance. Dr. S. P., a forestry professor at the university in the state's capital city, was a visionary leader and helped to establish eight hundred evangelistic agro-forestry societies across the state. Within a few years, the Foxes were reporting thousands of new believers among the Adivasi with a commensurate number of new churches.[3]

---

3. Erich Bridges, "Missionary Calvin Fox dies: helped end 'hunger season' for millions of Asians," in *Baptist Press*, December 18, 2003, https://www.baptistpress.com/resource-library/news/missionary-calvin-fox-dies-helped-end-hunger-season-for-millions-of-asians/.

When the Foxes began their work in 1995, there were 194 Baptist churches in the state with 10,030 members. History does not record how many of these churches were composed of Adivasi. Over the next eight years Fox would only report having personally helped to start seventy-five new Adivasi churches in 1999, a number that would grow to 232 churches by 2003. By the late 1990s, though, the Adivasi were starting new churches on their own. Fox estimated that the total number of Adivasi churches had grown from 1,215 in 1999 to 2,249 in 2023. The rapid and indigenous growth among the Adivasi prompted the IMB's area director to invite the Global Research Department in 2002 to conduct an assessment.

As the assessment was underway, Calvin Fox, who was on stateside assignment in the U.S., suffered a heart attack and passed away. In his eulogy of Fox, IMB executive vice president Clyde Meador said, "He led in outreach efforts that saw 100 churches become more than 2,000 churches in these last few years."[4]

Fox's passing ended the IMB's direct involvement with the Adivasi movement, but its indigenous growth continued well into the twenty-first century under the leadership of Dr. S. P. and the emerging Adivasi-led churches.

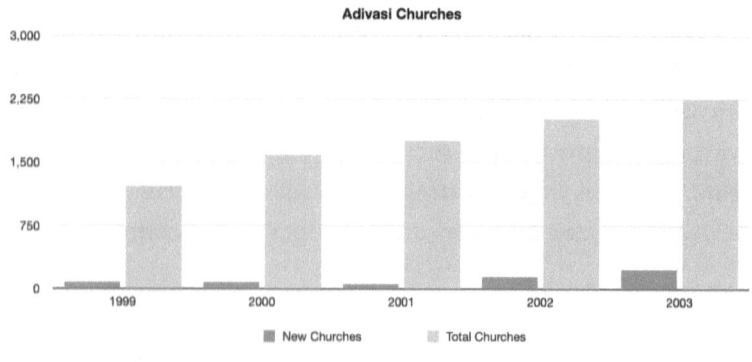

---

4. Bridges, "Missionary Calvin Fox dies."

The Adivasi Movement Assessment

In late 2001 and early 2002 Jim Slack began constructing a profile of the Adivasi in preparation for an on-site assessment. In March and April of 2003 Slack led an assessment team comprised of IMB South Asian missionaries Jeff Sundell and John Pettit, with IMB staff researcher Bill Shumaker, along with two additional unnamed IMB missionaries. To ensure objectivity, Slack and the regional leader for South Asia selected experienced missionaries who were not a part of the Adivasi work.

The team conducted 334 Adivasi interviews, some with groups of five to ten persons. Each interview lasted about two hours, and each person interviewed answered all of the team's 121 questions. Responses to the questions were captured verbatim and subsequently transferred to an Excel spreadsheet. The report also recorded that

> all of the questions were verbally asked through interpreters and the answers were written in notebooks or directly into a hardcopy version of the Excel spreadsheet. This was done for various cultural and technical reasons to ensure the integrity of the survey. It was not appropriate for us in this particular setting to use tape recorders or our computers in order to record the responses of those interviewed. The [resulting] Excel database covered 700 pages.

In terms of size, the assessment team concluded that the number of Baptist believers among the Adivasi had grown from 10,030 in 1995 to 127,080 baptized church members in 2002. These Adivasi Christians were worshipping in 2,017 churches with an additional 1,345 meeting in outreach groups. The team determined that 9,891 baptisms had already occurred in 2003. All of these factors were strong indicators of the vitality and future growth potential for the movement.

As was Slack's custom the team asked wide-ranging questions, including the informant's marital status; ordination as a pastor or deacon; whether mentored or discipled and by whom; questions about syncretism (whether the informant was still practicing former religious beliefs); apostasy from the faith; doctrinal issues; church polity issues; the practice of Communion and baptism; leadership training; distance from church site to where training took place; use of chronological Bible storying (including asking informants whether they could recite a story); literacy requirements for church planters in the movement; the availability of Scripture; local financial support of pastors; means of financing the work; sources of evangelistic influence; healing; ways of gathering a new church; and how long it takes to start a new church.

Slack observed, "There was a high level of response by those being interviewed, thus providing better accuracy and lowering the error factor." Thus, he concluded, "The error factor of the responses is placed accurately at between 3–5%." The assessment team's findings exceeded the four years of annual reports that the Foxes had submitted.

In October 2003 the assessment team issued an eight-page executive summary and seventy-seven-page confidential report on the work. Their conclusion was that a Church Planting Movement was well underway among the Adivasi.

The Hindu Basara People

Over the past century, movements to Christ among low-caste and tribal people groups in South Asia have been fairly common. However, work among high-caste Hindus has posed a much greater challenge.

The Basara people (the name we have given this people

group) was one of these high-caste Hindu sects, numbering approximately twenty million persons scattered across three South Asian states. In these states they wielded considerable political and societal influence. The Strategy Coordinators focused specifically on the nine million Basara living in their own state, where they were the largest of several Hindu sects, and the twelfth-largest unreached people group in the country. Due to their high-caste status and political power, most Christians had avoided outreach to the Basara.

This began to change in 1998 when a veteran Baptist missionary felt a calling to the Basara and initiated evangelistic outreach to them. Already fluent in the language, the missionaries immediately launched their Strategy Coordinator ministry. In addition to personal evangelistic efforts, the missionary began mobilizing other Christian ministries to engage the Basara.

In the first years of the ministry, the missionary worked with local partners to develop contextualized gospel literature tailored to the high-caste worldview of the Basara. Within a short time 300,000 gospel tracts were circulating among the Basara people.

To further expand the gospel's reach, the missionary launched a one-year, thirty-minute daily radio broadcast in the Basara language. The response to the broadcast was striking, with more than eight hundred responses, primarily from Basara listeners.

In 2001 the missionary reported three Basara churches were meeting regularly. The following year he reported sixteen new groups started with ninety baptized believers. In 2003 the number of churches and new groups had risen to forty-nine; and by 2004 he estimated 240 new groups were gathering with 900 new believers in discipleship.

That same year, the missionary and his regional leader began to assemble an assessment team to evaluate the scope and nature of the work.

The Basara Movement Assessment

By 2004 several regions of the world were reporting movements, and it was no longer possible for the Global Research Department to meet the growing demand for assessments. Thus, in 2004, the IMB's South Asia regional leader initiated an assessment of the Basara ministry. The assessment team consisted of two veteran IMB South Asia missionaries, Alan W. and Mark V., who ministered among other South Asian people groups. The team used an abbreviated form of Jim Slack's Church Planting Movement Assessment Guide as their instrument.

The team included in their assessment a profile of the Basara that the missionary had developed over the years. The missionary had crafted his first multipage profile as part of his Strategy Coordinator training prior to beginning his ministry.

Widespread interviews in Basara villages were not possible, so the team came up with a creative solution. They dropped into a conference of Basara Christian leaders without first announcing their intention to conduct interviews. Though the assessment team was able to gather fewer than twenty interviews, their findings were insightful. The team inquired as to how many believers were in each church; the typical size of a church; the number of outreach groups started by each church; how they were coming to Christ (individually or in family groups); how worship was conducted; the existence of syncretism; whether or not baptism and Communion were taking place; leadership training; location of the movement's members; and access to Scripture in the Basara language.

The team found that the Basara informants reflected an orthodox evangelical understanding of Christian doctrines, including the doctrines of salvation, baptism, and the Lord's Supper. However, they worshipped in a distinctly Basara manner. Rather than singing hymns, the Basara chanted poems that praised Jesus.

Communist, Berber, and Tribal Movements

Most of the Basara leaders who were interviewed related to multiple outreach groups and reported an average of thirty-five believers in their own ministry. Adopting Jim Slack's conservative "reduction formula," the team downsized their own estimate of the movement's size. Assuming that each of the two hundred Basara leaders at the conference represented fifteen to twenty-five Basara believers, the team agreed that the total number of Basara believers likely ranged from three- to five thousand.

The team then examined the number of churches among the Basara. They determined that even though the number of Basara outreach groups could be as high as three hundred, the number of established churches was perhaps no more than thirty, as many of the new believers had not yet been baptized due to community pressures.

A subsequent survey of the Basara was conducted by the South Asian Baptist Society, a group of local church planters who were not directly involved in the Basara work. Members of the Society surveyed 101 villages across the state, inquiring as to the existence and nature of emerging Christianity among the Basara. The Society reported numerous Basara Christian families, further corroborating the assessment team's findings.

Was the Basara work a Church Planting Movement? Perhaps not yet, but it reflected what was possible when a missionary with a vision for reaching a neglected people was deployed. The assessment team left open the question, but the data they gathered provided valuable insights into the ways the gospel was spreading among a previously neglected high-caste Hindu people group.

The Bhow Tribal People

The Bhow are a tribal people group numbering more than fifteen million, scattered across two countries and eight states in South

Asia. As conversion activities are highly restricted in the country where the Bhow people reside, we have anonymized their name as well as the names of those working among them. The Bhow speak several nonliterate languages and have lived for centuries on the fringes of South Asian society where they are often regarded as outlaws.

In the early 2000s IMB missionary Bruce Carlton began training a number of South Asian missionaries to adopt unreached people groups and function as Strategy Coordinators among them. One of these South Asian Strategy Coordinators, whom we'll call Batu, adopted the Bhow people and soon began to see a number of new believers and churches planted among them.

Batu reported significant growth among the Bhow people: 239 churches planted in 2002; 581 in 2003; 1,045 in 2004; and 1,725 in the first 10 months of 2005. He estimated the total number of Bhow believers had risen from about 3,000 in 2002 to more than 50,000 in 2005. Owing to their distance from direct involvement in the Bhow ministry, IMB missionaries relating to Batu were more cautious in the estimates they submitted in their annual reports.

In 2005, at Batu's invitation, the regional South Asia office began assembling a Church Planting Movement assessment team to evaluate the Bhow ministry.

The Bhow Movement Assessment

In October 2005 the CPM assessment team began their survey of Batu's reported movement among the Bhow people. The team consisted of twelve IMB South Asian missionaries, assisted by church planters from the South Asian Baptist Society, none of whom had been involved directly in the Bhow ministry.

The team traveled onsite and "dropped into" a Bhow Bible Conference, where they gathered 207 interviews (81 percent men, 19 percent women). This unannounced visit aimed at gaining candid responses from informants. The assessment team's interviews had five key objectives: (1) help other CPM practitioners learn how they could evaluate their work and implement principles and practices learned; (2) identify effective strategies and practices that could benefit other work; (3) describe and evaluate the faith and practice of churches within the movement; (4) provide feedback to the leaders of the movement to suggest any interventions needed to address current issues or avert future ones; (5) accurately describe the history, nature, and extent of the movement.

Drawing from the Global Research Team's CPM assessment questionnaire, the team explored conversions to Christianity; baptism; gender; marital status; age; when believers came to faith; leadership; vocation; income level; education; rural/urban; external funding; location of church; means of evangelism; how churches are planted; nature of discipleship; church planter training; leadership training; church polity; church meeting places; Lord's Supper and baptism; Bible teaching; worship styles; church music; reproduction rate of churches; and growth rate of the movement.

Regarding the movement's size, the assessment team found that Batu had likely underreported the extent of the growth. However, they also uncovered a significant disparity between the number of believers and those who had been baptized.

In 2002 the team found that of the 3,715 new believers, only 1,309 had been baptized. The following year 12,376 new believers were reported; yet only 5,019 had been baptized. In 2004 24,801 new believers were counted with only 8,990 having received baptism. Then, in 2005, the team identified 42,190 new believers but only 17,652 had been baptized.

Although the growth in new believers was noteworthy, the high number of unbaptized believers was a point of concern. The team estimated that the total number of believers had increased from 3,715 in 2002 to 83,082 in October 2005. However, only 39.7 percent or 32,970 of these new believers had been baptized.

These findings prompted Batu to make strategic adjustments to ensure a movement that would last. It was evident that the gospel was finding fertile soil among the Bhow; but without addressing the baptism issue, many new believers were not being assimilated into churches, which left them ill-equipped to grow in their Christian faith.

The assessment team also drilled deeply into questions of doctrinal integrity, ecclesiology, and leadership training. The broad input from 207 informants led the team to conclude that a Church Planting Movement was underway, but much refinement of the work remained to be done.

The Kekchi of Guatemala

The Kekchi, descendants of Guatemala's pre-Columbian Mayan people, reside primarily in the Peten and Alta Verapaz Departments, deep within the rugged interior of the country. In 2005 the Kekchi had a population of approximately 850,000. The Kekchi practiced a syncretistic blend of Catholicism and Mayan traditional religion. The remoteness of the Kekchi region insulated them from Guatemala's dominant Spanish-speaking society, and access to the gospel, as most of the Kekchi spoke no Spanish.

In 1964 Southern Baptist missionaries Ted and Sue Lindwall relocated to Cobán, the capital of Alta Verapaz, and began exploring ways to reach the Kekchi. The Lindwalls soon found the answer through a partnership with Neil Goss, an American dentist from Florida. Goss freely offered his services to the Kekchi, while Lindwall shared the gospel with them through an interpreter. In early 1965 the Lindwalls saw their first Kekchi come to faith in Christ and soon started the first Kekchi Baptist church. Before a medical crisis in 1966 forced the Lindwalls' departure from Cobán, missionaries Dick and Lahoma Greenwood joined the work, followed soon after by Don and Jane Courtney. Then, in 1971, they added Wendall and Jane Parker to their Kekchi missionary band.

Shortly after his arrival in 1966, Dick Greenwood declared, "I will never preach another sermon until I can do so in Kekchi." This commitment became a core value as the work progressed. Unlike many parts of Central America, the isolation of the Kekchi required the missionaries to depend upon the Kekchi to advance the work, rather than calling upon volunteers from the U.S.

The 1980s saw a resurgence of Mayan culture in the region, and the Baptist commitment to the Kekchi language rode the wave of that momentum as the response to the gospel increased. Between 1993 and 2004 Baptist work among the Kekchi experienced steady growth. In 1993 the missionaries reported 83 Kekchi congregations. By 2004 the number had risen to 370 churches, an increase of 346 percent.

Over the same eleven-year span, the reported number of baptized Kekchi believers grew from 9,457 to approximately 34,000, with up to 56,000 attending weekly church services. Over the same period the missionaries' report of annual baptisms increased from 373 in 1993 to 4,750 in 2004.

After several years of annual statistical reports indicating significant church growth among the Kekchi, the IMB's Global Research Department was invited to conduct a survey of the work.

The Kekchi Movement Assessment

In 2004 the IMB's Central America regional leader, Phil Templin, formally requested an assessment of the Kekchi ministry. After compiling substantial historical, demographic, and missionary research on the Kekchi, the Slack-led team set out for Central America in January 2005. Their survey would extend into the following month. Slack's team consisted of three IMB missionaries (Dennis Jones, Donald Barger, and Alan Lyons). These men all served as missionaries in other Spanish-speaking countries. They were assisted by local, bilingual translators from the Kekchi Baptist community. To widen the perspective, Slack invited Southwestern Seminary mission professor and church growth specialist Dr. Daniel Sanchez to join the assessment team.

Over several weeks in January and February 2005, the team made the best attempt to date at securing random samplings of informants. They began with a list of all known Kekchi churches and then randomly selected churches from the list. The team sought the following informant demographics: (a) a 2:1 lay to pastor ratio; (b) one-third to one-half of the informants were to be women, though Kekchi women were not as accessible for outsiders to interview; (c) no informants under the age of 12 were interviewed; and (d) a target of 1–5 percent of the total number of Kekchi churches was to be assessed.

Although the team aspired to interview 275 Kekchi informants, they ultimately completed 260 interviews. In addition to these Kekchi Christians, the team interviewed Baptist and non-Baptist missionaries such as the Wycliffe Bible translators working among the Kekchi.

The assessment team learned that Wycliffe missionaries, Ruth Carlson and Frances Euchus, were unsung heroes of much that had happened among the Kekchi. Carlson and Euchus had been living among the Kekchi since 1955 and had advocated for missionary engagement of this neglected people. It was from Carlson and Euchus that subsequent missionaries received their first lessons in the Kekchi language.

The team discovered that while the Kekchi movement had benefited from Wycliffe's translation of Scripture, greater impact came as Bible stories were translated into songs. Hymns and Christian songs in the Kekchi language had been particularly effective in embedding the gospel message in the hearts of the people.

The assessors were impressed by the indigenous nature of the Kekchi movement, noting that "home services have been a major contributing growth factor among the Kekchi.... Strong congregations have developed from home service beginnings." They observed that almost every new church start began in a home; and by the time they became a congregation, these new church starts provided their own building from their own resources. This self-reliance was in stark contrast to the pattern throughout much of Central America where Christians relied upon volunteer teams from the U.S. to construct their church buildings.

The assessment report cited the decision by the missionaries to minister in the Kekchi language as pivotal to their success. Choosing to minister in Kekchi rather than Spanish, the language of the landowners and government, had been criticized by some within the Spanish-speaking Guatemala Baptist Mission, government officials, and local landowners. One of the CPM assessment team members commented: "This was the most significant choice that the first missionaries made. If they had not made this choice, I do not think that the Gospel would have spread as naturally as it did."

In the conclusion to their 62-page confidential report, the team affirmed that the Kekchi ministry was a Church Planting Movement. They determined that 83 churches in 1993 had grown to 370 churches in 2004. Baptized Kekchi believers in those churches over the same time period had grown from 9,457 to at least 34,000. Likewise, the number of annual baptisms had risen from 373 in 1993 to 4,750 in 2004. As the team viewed the churches' 513 new outreach groups with 10,891 attending, they predicted the continuing growth of indigenous church multiplication among the Kekchi people.

Concluding Observations

The movements depicted above were complex and unpredictable. Despite many shared characteristics, each movement was unique and did not fit into traditional patterns of church growth. They did, however, contain most if not all of the qualities that were first described in the Church Planting Movements profiled in 1999. These assessed movements confirmed the emergence of Church Planting Movements as a new phenomenon—one that differed significantly from traditional missionary church planting.

When these field reports of movements began arriving at the International Mission Board's headquarters, they were met initially with skepticism. However, rather than dismissing them, the IMB's Global Research Department determined to investigate further.

Still on the horizon were Church Planting Movements in urban centers, and that is the subject of the next chapter.

SEVEN

CAN CHURCH PLANTING MOVEMENTS OCCUR IN CITIES?

One of the common myths about Church Planting Movements is that they do not occur in cities. Even today, a quarter century after the first movements appeared, one hears that CPMs are a rural phenomenon, a village thing. If this is true, then CPMs hold little promise for a rapidly urbanizing world. In fact, as we will see in this chapter, Church Planting Movements are taking place in urban settings.

Most cities, even in the least-Christian corners of the world, have some sort of Christian presence. Oftentimes these churches are remnants of a colonial age when missionary church planting, with its accompanying establishment of buildings and pastors, was still legal. Today, when these church buildings survive, they are seen as monuments to a bygone era and scrutinized closely by the postcolonial government.

Can Church Planting Movements take root is such environments? This was the challenge embraced by the IMB's urban missionaries as they entered the twenty-first century.

By the early 2000s IMB Strategy Coordinators were engaging scores of unreached cities, most with populations between two and ten million. For many of these urban missionaries, their preferred methodology was Training for Trainers (T4T). They favored this approach for its rapid indigenization that resulted in viral evangelism, immediate discipleship, and new church formation. Because T4T was lay-led and usually took place in homes, it functioned discretely and evaded government opposition. For the same reasons it also contextualized naturally and integrated the gospel into the communities of its practitioners.

Each of the urban ministries described in this chapter was taking place in a country that remains quite hostile to Christian missional activity. As a result, the identities of the locations and individuals involved must remain anonymous.

Wu City and Environs

Wu City is a provincial capital that had a population of about eight million in 2006. Though there were some fifty ethnic minorities in the city, the great majority of the population shared a common language and ethnicity. The history of missionary work in Wu City traced back to the great Protestant missionary enterprise of the nineteenth and early twentieth centuries. War and political change saw the expulsion of all foreign missionaries from the country in the mid-twentieth century.

By the early 2000s missionaries were beginning to reenter the country with non-missionary visas. As they arrived they discovered that government persecution had succeeded in stifling Christian growth and activity.

As part of their Strategy Coordinator training, the IMB missionary couple to Wu City did extensive pre-field research, examining the city's economic, historic, linguistic, religious, and

Can Church Planting Movements Occur in Cities?

cultural distinctives. Their training also investigated best practices in Church Planting Movements, gleaned from case studies from a variety of settings. Upon arriving in Wu City around the year 2002, the missionaries visited existing churches and believing communities to further their understanding.

In 2003 the missionary launched his first T4T training in Wu City. By 2006 the missionary was reporting three separate streams of multiplying disciples and new church starts.[1]

As new disciples in the first stream of work implemented T4T, they started a significant number of new churches. The missionary reported fourteen new churches started in 2003, seventeen new churches in 2004, and twenty-five new churches in 2005. By 2006 the missionary was reporting a total of fifty-six house churches across the first T4T stream of ministry.

The second stream was launched in a suburban area near Wu City. In 2003 the missionary conducted his first T4T training. Two new church starts soon followed. Then, in 2004, they started another three groups, with four new T4T home groups added in 2005. By the first quarter of 2006, an additional seven new church starts were underway.

The third stream was located in a different area near Wu City and was led by the missionary's 44-year-old partner named Jou. Jou had been a member of the state-sanctioned church since coming to faith in 2001. In the spring of 2003 the government closed Jou's church, which prompted him to join a house church where he received the missionary's T4T training. By the end of that year Jou and his band of T4T practitioners had started three new churches. In 2004 they added nine new churches, and the

---

1. In addition to heavy reliance upon prayer and biblical instruction, Ying's ecclesiology included tithing and offerings. This key practice stemmed from his own experience as a pastor and son of a pastor. In movements following this T4T model, the inclusion of tithes and offerings had the benefit of freeing the emerging church networks from dependence upon external funding.

Strategy Coordinator reported personally baptizing more than 100 new believers.[2] In 2005 the stream added an additional nine house churches. At the time of the 2006 CPM assessment, the third stream was reporting a total of twenty-one emerging churches with around 250 believers.

Alongside the planting of new churches, the missionary tracked the ongoing discipleship of new believers. In 2003 the missionary reported 410 baptisms, but only 380 church members participating in discipleship training. The following year the number of baptisms rose to 593 but only 258 persons in discipleship training. Then, in 2005, as the missionary made adjustments to his strategy, the stream added 589 newly baptized believers, while church discipleship training increased to 950. In 2006 the work added 634 newly baptized believers with 1,580 believers engaged in discipleship training. By 2008 the missionary reported 830 baptisms with 1,700 persons receiving discipleship training in their church.

In the spring of 2006 the IMB's Asia regional leader assembled a CPM assessment team to visit Wu City and assess the health and scope of the work.

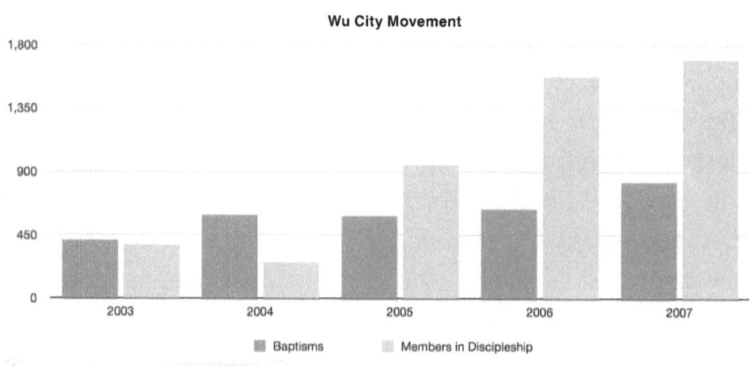

---

2. As Church Planting Movement aficionados will note, baptism by outsiders is generally counterproductive to Church Planting Movements, and the assessment team subsequently flagged this as a point of concern.

Can Church Planting Movements Occur in Cities?

The Assessment of Wu City and Environs

Between March 28 and April 1, 2006, the IMB's Asia regional office deployed an onsite team to assess the ministry in Wu City. Though the team produced an extensive confidential survey of the work in Wu city, only a three-page executive summary survives.[3]

The assessment began with the Strategy Coordinator's urban profile and the monthly reports he had submitted since arriving in the city. The onsite assessment surveyed both the missionary's work and that of the historic Wu City churches. This comparison provided the team with a context for evaluating methods and effectiveness.

The team found that earlier Presbyterian missionaries had established churches with buildings, pastors, elders, and members who defended their faith from state-sanctioned opposition. From their interviews of the older churches, the team discovered that though the government had allowed these churches to persist, they had experienced little growth over the preceding decades. Years of resistance to anti-Christian pressures had also left the local Christians suspicious of the new expressions of Christianity that were emerging around them. When asked about the reasons for their opposition to the new evangelistic movement, more than one informant criticized "excessive pressure to share" one's faith.

The assessment team then turned their attention to the three T4T streams of new churches that the missionary had reported. Tight government constraints limited the number of informants the team could interview. Nonetheless, they managed to visit all

---

3. The pattern of destroying the extensive confidential assessment report was common in this Asian region where government hostility against Christianity was a continual threat. Prior to its destruction, however, the regional leadership and Strategy Coordinator would glean whatever insights and recommendations it offered.

three of the streams. The team interviewed twelve informants from the first stream, four from the second, and seven from the third.

The informants the team interviewed confirmed the numbers in the missionary's report. They also stated that many of the Christians from the traditional churches were suspicious of and even actively slowing the new work. Traditional churches, which typically required three years to raise up new leaders, questioned the rapid T4T growth and its immediate reliance upon new Christians with little formal theological education.

In their report the assessment team confirmed that the IMB's missionary in the city had either started or contributed to ninety-three new church starts over a three-year period of time. An emerging movement was under way. Nonetheless, the team noted that the work had not yet reached a tipping point that would ensure sufficient momentum to reach the entire city. However, they were optimistic about the trajectory of the ministry. Citing the prayer-saturated biblical methods of T4T, and the resurgence in church-based discipleship training, the team expressed confidence in the ministry's prospects moving forward.

Lo City

With an urban population of roughly four million, Lo City was largely homogeneous, with only a scattering of small ethnic enclaves. In the fall of 2003 the IMB assigned a missionary to serve as Strategy Coordinator for Lo City. At the inception of his ministry, the Strategy Coordinator identified several traditional churches and one house church. Given the government restrictions on new church buildings, the missionary determined that the viral methodology of T4T offered the best prospects for reaching Lo City's millions.

Can Church Planting Movements Occur in Cities?

At the end of 2004 the missionary reported twenty new T4T-based house churches in Lo City. By the end of 2005 the missionary was reporting seventy new house-church plants. By mid 2006, despite some attrition, the missionary conservatively estimated a total of eighty-five churches in Lo City.

The discrepancy between church starts and total churches reflected the fact that not all of the church starts had matured into churches. The rapid church growth in Lo City was posing challenges for the new Christians. The missionary struggled to find sufficient leaders to keep pace with the rapidly multiplying network of new churches. However, as new disciples proved themselves faithful, he developed a core group of six local partners, each training a second tier of leaders, who in turn trained others.

In his monthly reports, the missionary expressed concern over tensions that had arisen between the new house churches and the older state-sanctioned churches, prompting a visit from an onsite coaching and assessment team.

Lo City Assessment

Between April 28 and May 1, 2006 an assessment team discretely traveled to Lo City to conduct an onsite survey. In addition to a three-page executive summary, the assessment team produced an extensive confidential report that no longer survives.

The 2006 assessment team was able to confirm the existence of only forty-two of the seventy house groups the missionary had identified in his 2005 annual report. The team interviewed eighteen informants from these emerging churches to identify strengths and weaknesses of the work.

The assessment team affirmed the vision that had captivated the new believers, citing the six-member team of local T4T leaders. These local partners had developed a plan to reach 750,000 persons in their city over the next three years, with measurable goals of evangelizing 5,000 each week. This would allow them to reach 250,000 annually over the next three years. Among the weaknesses they identified was a deficit in sufficient leaders to shepherd the growing number of new disciples and groups.

The assessment team was not yet ready to call the Lo City work a Church Planting Movement. In their concluding observations they described the work as "an emerging Church Planting Movement," which still had many challenges to overcome.

So City

In the early 2000s So City had a population of nearly eight million, with more than twenty million in the surrounding districts. The city was multiethnic, though 91 percent of its inhabitants belonged to a single ethnolinguistic group. Baptist work began in So City in 1994, and the first church was planted the following year. In 2003 a new Strategy Coordinator completed his training and relocated to the city.

In 2004 the Strategy Coordinator launched his first T4T training. After an encouraging response, by the end of the year he reported several movement-threatening challenges. The greatest challenge was that despite many new believers coming to faith in Christ most were choosing to join neither the state-sanctioned churches nor the new house churches. One stream of work reported leading 4,000 people to faith between 2003 and 2004, yet only 150 were gathering in churches.

The missionary reported another stream had led more than 1,000 people to faith in Christ, yet only 110 were baptized. Reflecting further attrition, only a dozen of these newly baptized believers had been incorporated into churches.

By 2006 the missionary had launched sixteen different

streams of church planting activity in So City, but he was troubled by the lack of the new believers' assimilation into the house church network. In his monthly reports the missionary appealed to his supervisor for help. That same year the IMB's Asia regional leader deployed an assessment team to provide onsite coaching and counsel.

The So City Assessment

On May 8, 2006 the IMB's regional office deployed an assessment team to visit So City to examine the missionary's work. Over the next four days the team gathered thirty-two interviews drawn from eleven of the sixteen streams of church-planting activity in the city. The CPM assessment team subsequently produced a three-page executive summary of their findings.

The team confirmed many of the problems the missionary had reported, and they explored further. They determined that five of the streams lacked clear biblical faith and practice. As an explanation they noted that four of these five were still following the registered churches' practice of baptism by sprinkling, which likely indicated the existence of infant baptism rather than believer's baptism.

The survey team observed that one of the house-church streams insisted that only a representative from the registered church was authorized to baptize new believers. This dependence on the registered church pastors limited the new house churches' ability to function as autonomous churches that could reproduce into a movement.

The team determined that the state-sponsored church was functioning as a gatekeeper in the city. While the state-sponsored church's good reputation had contributed to the positive reception of the gospel, its model of pastor-led, building-based institutions was also slowing the reproduction of new disciples and churches.

Additionally, the team discovered that many of the new house churches were actually functioning as cell-churches. These cell churches remained under the governance of the state-sanctioned mother churches whose leaders provided both Communion and baptism.

Eight other assessed streams were described as "baptistic," or autonomous, in their church polity but had little vision for a Church Planting Movement. Many informants expressed uncertainty about whether to affiliate with the government-sanctioned church or shift to house churches. Other informants reported engagement in a wide range of good, but not-CPM-oriented, Western programs such as *Experiencing God* or *Purpose-Driven Church* models.

Most troubling to the team was the discovery that despite an unusual responsiveness to the gospel, significant numbers of new believers were not being incorporated into churches. The problem was so acute that "one house church group noted that they have decided not to continue doing evangelism due to their inability to conserve the fruit."

The assessment team highlighted three general concerns with the work in So City: (1) significant numbers of new believers were not being incorporated into groups, (2) a majority of the streams were starting cell groups rather than churches, and (3) even among streams that were apparently biblical in faith and practice, they lacked a vision for starting new churches.

In conclusion, although the people of So City were quite open to the gospel and expressed a willingness to follow Christ, their response did not result in church membership where ongoing discipleship could take place. As a result, many of these converts drifted away. In short, a Church Planting Movement had not yet emerged.

The team determined, since the missionary had only begun to use T4T the previous year, it was premature to evaluate the effect T4T would have in subsequent years. The assessment team's suggestions prompted the Strategy Coordinator to modify his training to strengthen the emphasis on church as the locus for Christian maturation.

Co City

Co City was a provincial capital and major industrial hub located at the confluence of two rivers. When an IMB Strategy Coordinator located there, around the year 2000, the urban complex had a growing population of more than ten million.

In 2001 and 2002 the Strategy Coordinator reported two new churches started each year. In 2003 the number increased to four new church starts. Then, as he implemented T4T, he saw a marked upturn. In 2004 he reported starting forty-five new house churches. Then, in 2005, those he had trained started seventy-one new churches for a total of 108 churches in the city. By the end of 2006 the missionary had seen an additional eighty-three new church starts for a total of 153 churches spread across nine streams of outreach. His monthly reports indicated that about 70 percent of the new church starts had come as a direct result of T4T training.

In 2006 the missionary reached out to his supervisor with a request for onsite coaching and a CPM assessment. The following year the IMB's Asia regional leader deployed a Church Planting Movement assessment team to Co City.

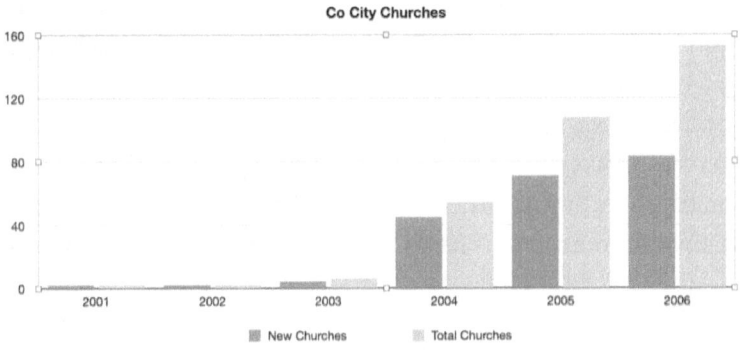

The Co City Assessment

In April 2007, a four-member assessment team, consisting of two male and two female missionaries, was deployed by the IMB's regional office to conduct an onsite visit to Co City.

The team conducted their interviews in a business-district hotel to avoid government attention. They interviewed forty-seven informants in twenty-three interview sessions. The informants represented eight of the nine streams of house-church multiplication. Of these informants, twenty-seven were female and twenty were male, with ages ranging from twenty-one to seventy-five.

The team asked each informant about (1) biographical background (age, vocation, testimony); (2) their role in the church; (3) what took place in their church service; (4) how they did evangelism; (5) leadership and leadership training; (6) their views on church multiplication; (7) challenges they faced; (8) miracles they had experienced or witnessed; and (9) their vision for the work. Each of these nine fields of inquiry included several sub-questions.

The team noted that two of the topics, "#6, Multiplication" and "#8, Miracles" received the least enthusiastic response from the informants. The Strategy Coordinator had inserted the question about miracles; he sensed that if his local partners did not believe in God's power to do the miraculous, they would struggle to believe that a Church Planting Movement was possible. However, the assessment team concluded it was the absence of a vision for multiplication, rather than the absence of miracles, that was hindering the emergence of a Church Planting Movement.

The team determined that even though most of the lay Christians were evangelizing, most did not yet feel capable of starting new churches themselves. While participatory Bible study was common in the T4T streams, the majority of the new

Can Church Planting Movements Occur in Cities?

believers continued to look to professional pastors to preach the Bible.

When the assessment team interviewed members of state-sanctioned churches, they discovered that tithes and offerings were channeled into maintaining their meeting places rather than starting new house churches. This contrasted sharply with the T4T groups that were situated in homes and focused on starting new groups. The team did find encouragement, though, in the growing number of T4T-spawned house churches that were built around lay-led participatory Bible study and the making of new disciples.

In their thirty-five-page report, the team acknowledged the Co City work was on track to become a Church Planting Movement, despite many challenges still to be overcome. Their onsite observations provided the missionary with recommendations as he sought to steer the work toward an ongoing movement.

Even as these urban ministries grappled with the challenge of multiplication, their assessments provided invaluable tools for coaching, correction, and accountability. The assessments identified obstacles, offered ways forward, and provided encouragement and coaching to each of the missionaries.

An Asian Megalopolis Movement

This vast urban area, deemed a megalopolis, consists of nine cities that have virtually grown together with a combined population of more than eighty million. It was into this vast urban sprawl that the IMB deployed veteran missionaries, Ying and Grace Kai, in 1999.

The Kais, who were introduced to the reader in chapter four, were children of Asian Baptists. Ying's father had been a pastor and church planter in Taiwan, and Ying continued his father's legacy. After immigrating to the United States and pastoring a church in Texas for several years, the Kais felt God's calling to return to Asia as missionaries with the International Mission Board.

The Kais began their missionary career in an open city in Asia where Ying pastored a traditional church and planted a number of new churches. In the late 1990s the Kais sensed God's calling to the unreached and requested a transfer to an under-engaged mission field. In 1999 they received their new assignment and were trained as Strategy Coordinators to the rapidly growing megalopolis where their new ministry would unfold.

The Kais realized quickly that despite their fluency in the language and gifting in evangelism, personally planting churches one by one could never reach all of the megacity's eighty million persons. Out of this realization of their personal limitations the Kais developed what came to be known as T4T or Training for Trainers.[4]

The premise of T4T was to evangelize widely and immediately train those led to Christ to become evangelists, trainers, and church-planter trainers themselves. The resulting T4T endeavor proved far more effective than the Kais could have imagined.

The Kais launched their first T4T training in October 2000. By January 2001 their band of trainees had already started twenty small groups that were becoming churches. By May of that year there were 327 small groups and 4,000 newly baptized believers. New churches were soon scattered across seventeen towns. By the end of 2001 the Kais' network of T4T-trained partners reported 908 house churches with more than 12,000 new Christians.

The following year, the Kais' T4T network saw 3,535 new

---

4. See Steve Smith with Ying Kai, *T4T: A Discipleship Re-Revolution* (Monument, CO: WIGTake Resources, 2011) or Ying and Grace Kai, *Ying and Grace Kai's Training for Trainers* (Monument, CO: WIGTake Resources, 2017).

churches planted with approximately 53,430 baptisms. Then, in the first six months of 2003, the movement reported an additional 9,320 new churches and conducted 104,542 baptisms.[5] By 2003 Ying was personally training 300–400 church planters each month. In addition to his direct training, the work cascaded through fifteen proficient "big trainers," spread across thirty training centers. These training centers met in homes, hotels, and restaurants, as well as in government-sanctioned churches.

By 2004 the Kais' supervisor had received forty-two monthly reports, and was aware of the growing numbers that the Kais were reporting. Grace Kai had meticulously tracked the growing work, documenting each evangelistic outreach, training event, and new church plant. She also tracked the subsequent generations of new outreaches, training events, and church starts that streamed from their initial efforts.

The Kais' numbers were unprecedented in the IMB. Consequently, in 2004, the IMB's regional leader invited an assessment team to survey the work in the urban megalopolis.

The Megalopolis Movement Assessment

In September 2004 veteran IMB missionary Dr. Bill Smith led an assessment team to evaluate the Church Planting Movement reports from Ying and Grace Kai. The team included fluent-language speaker Jim Courson, Dr. Jim Haney (director of the IMB's Global Research Department), and Ying and Grace Kai, who were fluent in two of the local languages spoken within the movement. Over twelve days the team traveled extensively

---

5. These extraordinary numbers proved to be an understatement of what occurred in the megalopolis movement.

through the urban megalopolis and a neighboring province to investigate the reported church multiplication.

Ying Kai was uneasy about the assessment, not because he doubted the movement, but because of increasing government opposition. As the summary later noted, "Three months prior to the CPM evaluation, five pastors and one official responsible for controlling religion were jailed for failing to curtail the rapid spread of Christianity." The outside assessors reassured Ying of their sensitivity to his concerns, and they discussed how to proceed cautiously.

Working closely with the Kais, the team agreed on the following guidelines for their survey:

1. Select representatively (i.e., obtain a random sampling)—to gather information from representative pastors, trainers, students, farmers, and others
2. Meet securely—in venues and times selected by their hosts
3. Dialogue comfortably—going with what was given in the course of conversation and expanding without heavy question and answer sessions (i.e., avoid sounding like interrogators)
4. Listen carefully—without taking notes (during the interviews)
5. Write immediately—recording verbatim notes as soon and as completely as possible after the interview sessions

As Smith acknowledged in his executive summary, "When the CPM gets large, tracking and confirming the total extent of the movement becomes beyond capability in a restricted access area." Nonetheless, the team made a valiant effort. Over the 12-day assessment, the team conducted 400 to 500 interviews in

Can Church Planting Movements Occur in Cities?

multiple languages. Informants included literate and nonliterate, individuals and groups, factory workers and owners, house churches and members of an open megachurch, where 1,200 to 1,500 members had been trained in T4T. The team estimated more than half of the informants were female.[6]

The survey began by analyzing the Kais' forty-two monthly reports of churches and training events. The team plotted the location of each of these churches and training venues on maps. The sheer number of churches was overwhelming. The team then randomly selected church and training venues for onsite interviews. To circumvent security challenges they conducted the interviews in hotel rooms, restaurants, minivans with shaded windows, training centers, government-sanctioned churches, and residential apartments.

In each instance the survey corroborated the Kais' reports. In their executive summary, the team confirmed in the Kais' work "an extraordinary movement of God"—even by Church Planting Movement standards. The multiple streams of T4T-based new churches had produced thousands of reproducing new believers, disciples, and churches.

Ying had treated each new disciple as a fellow trainer, and the team found these trainers had been instrumental in planting at least 44,096 new churches with an estimated 483,235 baptized believers. Though some of the new believers were members of traditional, state-sanctioned churches, the majority met in their own apartment homes. The average church size was found to be just under eleven members.

One of the house churches the team interviewed was the product of twenty generations of reproduction from the original

---

6. While most of the information in this section on the megalopolis movement assessment was drawn directly from the team's 88-page confidential report, additional information was collected in a follow-up interview with two of the assessment team members.

training event. Though this house church did not know Ying Kai, they were using the precise training material and methods that had been introduced by Ying and reproduced faithfully twenty times before reaching them.

The assessment team confirmed the twenty generations of reproduction after first observing the T4T methods the twentieth-generation house church was using, then asking them, "Who led you to Christ and trained you? Who trained them?" This took them back several generations. They then asked the Kais, "Who did the T4T training in this area, and whom did they report having trained?" This also extended multiple generations until they found the overlap with the twentieth generation of reproducing T4T evangelism, discipleship, and church formation.

In addition to their numerical assessment, the team examined the doctrinal integrity of the training materials the Kais were using. Topics covered in the interviews included (1) personal information about the informant (language, gender, education level, location of residence, languages spoken, length of time a believer, role in the church), (2) church practice and doctrine, (3) role of Scripture, (4) role of prayer, (5) persecution, (6) durability of churches, (7) charismatic practices, (8) nature and extent of syncretism, (9) faith and practice (including baptism, the Lord's Supper, and church discipline), and (10) leadership training.

Upon the assessment team's return to the U.S., they produced an eighty-eight-page confidential report of their findings and delivered a five-page executive summary to the International Mission Board's leadership. In the course of their onsite investigation, the team determined that the Kais had actually been underreporting to the IMB home office, by about 40 percent, the actual number of new believers and churches.

When asked why he had underreported his numbers, Ying explained:

Can Church Planting Movements Occur in Cities?

Some of those we've trained were from denominations with the practice of baptizing infants and we know that the IMB does not consider those to be valid, so we didn't report these streams of churches. In some of the factory compounds, the workers were all women, and they started many churches. We know that the IMB has some problems with women leading churches, so we did not report these churches to the IMB headquarters.[7]

By mid-2004, the team estimated that more than 485,000 persons had come to Christ through the Kais' T4T initiative, resulting in more than 44,000 new church starts. The movement had spread through multiple streams that stretched across all nine cities of the megalopolis and even spilled into a neighboring province.

The Kais continued their work until 2010 then shifted to a global training role. At the time of the couple's departure from the Asian megalopolis, the IMB could trace 1.7 million baptisms to the Kais' T4T ministry and determined that approximately 150,000 new churches had been started.

On their official website the IMB later noted: "Ying and Grace saw unprecedented growth in the number of churches and Christians in East Asia. It exceeded any church growth the IMB has seen in its 175-year history, and it still continues today."[8]

In the years that followed, the simple strategy of Training for Trainers spread to many countries. Movement catalysts found that T4T's insistence upon routine follow-up made it easy to track the effectiveness of trainees. By regularly reconvening

---

7. Quote obtained in a phone conversation with one of the assessment team members in a follow-up interview, July 12, 2024.

8. See "Ying and Grace Kai," International Mission Board, https://www.imb.org/175/missionary-profiles/ying-grace-kai/?returnto=ying-and-grace-kai&pageid=127438, accessed April 11, 2024.

individuals from these training groups, the missionary could determine who was a true disciple of Christ, what Ying Kai called "a doer of the Word and not a hearer only."[9] The fruit of genuine discipleship was evident in the ongoing implementation of evangelism, discipleship, and church formation, with each trainee passing on these principles to others.

Concluding Observations

These urban Church Planting Movement assessments dispel the notion that movements cannot occur in cities. While urban work is distinct from rural CPM efforts, these distinctions can be understood and addressed through thorough assessments, even when faced with security threats and opposition posed by other churches.

It is in the quest to overcome these challenges that new breakthroughs often occur. One of these urban breakthroughs that became a gift to the entire church was Ying and Grace Kai's Training for Trainers.

---

9. Lest the Kais' definition of a true disciple be dismissed as pragmatism, consider its source. James 1:22 says, "But be doers of the word, and not hearers only, deceiving yourselves" (ESV).

EIGHT

YES, THERE WERE ALSO NON-MOVEMENTS

Someone once said that a negative cannot be disproved. If this is true, how can we determine when a purported Church Planting Movement is not, in fact, a Church Planting Movement?

Wouldn't it be strange if every time an assessment team set out to evaluate a movement they always found one? Researchers call this confirmation bias. Confirmation bias occurs when we search for, interpret, or remember information in a way that confirms our preexisting beliefs or theories, rather than evaluating the evidence objectively.

A robust assessment should be capable of uncovering not only what is present but also what is absent. In this chapter we will explore several assessed ministries that even though thought to be Church Planting Movements, turned out to be something else.

Revisiting the Bangladeshi Muslim Movement

In chapter five, we examined two Bengali Muslim-background movements with more than 93,000 converts to the Christian faith. In 2003 Kevin Greeson, who helped to catalyze one of the Bangladeshi movements, transferred to a neighboring country to assume a new region-wide role. When he left Bangladesh, Greeson transferred his responsibilities to his Bangladeshi partner.

The Bangladeshi partner was soon reporting even greater growth in new believers and churches. By the end of 2004 he had counted nearly 24,000 total churches with more than half a million baptized members. His report further claimed that more than 157,000 new Muslim-background converts had been baptized the previous year. If his numbers were correct, Bangladesh was now home to one of the fastest-growing Church Planting Movements in the world.

Encouraged by the valuable insights from the 2002 assessment, Greeson and his regional leader requested a new survey. The Global Research Department allocated ten thousand dollars to facilitate the effort.

The local Bangladeshi partner, however, was less enthusiastic about such an ambitious project. Nevertheless, at the urging of his IMB colleagues, he agreed to pull together a sampling of reporting churches and their leaders from across the country.

In the fall of 2004 the IMB's Jim Haney began forming an assessment team. With encouragement from the South Asia regional leader, Haney invited participation from each of the IMB's regions that had work among Muslims. He then expanded the team's composition to include participants from other agencies. The goal of expanding the team was to increase objectivity and allow others to learn from the movement.

To minimize confirmation bias, neither the current regional leader for South Asia nor the former Strategy Coordinator for the work served as members of the team, though the latter assisted as a liaison with his local Bangladeshi partner.

To manage the challenge of surveying an entire nation,

the team divided the country into its six political divisions and assigned a two-member team to each division.¹ The survey extended over ten days, but it didn't take long for problems to surface. Though the team noted the IMB missionaries had conducted themselves with transparency and integrity, something was awry. The local informants appeared to be scripted and coached, which led the assessors to suspect the Bangladeshi leader might be attempting to manipulate the survey.

How did the team arrive at their surprising conclusions? A glimpse into their confidential 2005 report tells the story.

When interviewers deviated from their questionnaire, some of the informants' testimonies disintegrated or became confused. Some of the surveyors questioned the plausibility of their informants' stories:

> On November 7 we interviewed twelve people who said they were county level evangelists/leaders, nine were men and three were women. The three women were 18, 18 and 14 years old. These three said that they had been church leaders since they came to faith in 2002.

This would have meant the three women were sixteen and twelve years old when they became church leaders. Though possible, it raised obvious questions.

---

1. The paired team members were: (1) Phil Parshall (veteran Bengali speaker, SIM missionary, and author of *New Paths in Muslim Evangelism*) with Elaine Meador (veteran missionary and wife of the former regional leader for South Asia); (2) Donald Crawford (veteran missionary from the Middle East) with Dr. George Tupper (veteran missionary and fluent Bengali speaker); (3) Don Allen (training director for the Muslim-mission organization Frontiers) with Joey Morrison (IMB missionary, fluent in Bengali); (4) Keith McKinley (who had grown up in Bangladesh) with Wes Johnson (IMB missionary, fluent in Bengali); (5) John Basham (IMB trainer from East Africa) with Randy Rains (former IMB missionary in Bangladesh); and (6) Everett Miller (IMB missionary in Bangladesh) with Steve Smith (missionary author of *T4T: A Discipleship Re-Revolution*).

The same team also found it odd that

there were no remarkable differences in their reports for their respective sections of the division. Everyone reported about the same number of churches and baptisms regardless of when the first church in their section had been started.

After conducting surveys in three cities, another pair of assessors noted:

A few of the more mature leaders were scattered among the group, and they persisted in brazenly "coaching" the others with answers, using such methods as body language, hand signals, and thinly-veiled whispers behind hand-covered mouths. As a result of the irregularities reported in the . . . interviews, our assessment team concludes that we do not have reliable numbers to report. . . .

Another team of assessors stated:

We have a commitment to the truth. Obviously, this is a happy and hard time for us. We are happy that the truth is coming out, but it is hard to do these kinds of audits. The movement could be huge; it's unfortunate that deception stood in the way of getting to what God is doing.

Yet another team commented, "We do not know if this is a CPM due to the lack of accurate statistics."

Not all of the assessment teams, however, came to the same conclusion. A minority report from another division stated,

In our division, we reported slightly less than 5,000 active churches and slightly more than 102,000 active believers.

Yes, There Were Also Non-Movements

At no time did we really feel we were being intentionally deceived, even in relation to the statistics received.

In the end, five of the six assessment teams concluded they had not received sufficient accurate information to determine the nature or extent of the movement. The team's report could not confirm that a movement or movements were *not* occurring; the absence of evidence was not evidence of absence. But the team almost unanimously determined that the input from the field informants and national leader had not been reliable.

It was a painful, yet sobering, experience. During the team's debriefing with the national leader, the leader was asked about the evidence of deception. He apologized to the CPM assessment team for not verifying the numbers reported, but he reiterated his reluctance to undertake such a massive survey. Prayer together led to restoration. Honest conversations began discussion of how, in the future, a true random sampling might be attempted to gain a more accurate picture of what was happening.

In January 2005 Jim Haney produced an eight-two-page confidential report and a fifteen-page executive summary of the teams' findings. While Haney reported that a Church Planting Movement or movements were possible and even probable, their size and nature could not be determined from this assessment.

In the report Haney noted, "Most felt that some kind of movement is going on." Unfortunately, its size and scope remained elusive. As a result of the 2004 assessment, though, the IMB returned to the more certain numbers gathered in 2002. The 2002 assessment had gathered random interviews from 150 informants with 27 areas of inquiry. It had confirmed in Bangladesh the existence of two movement networks with approximately 395 local evangelists; 2,439 pastors; 3,138 churches; and 93,453 members.

Though the movements in Bangladesh had likely grown since 2002, the IMB's published numbers would not be speculated upon nor updated. Instead, the Bangladesh numbers would remain at their 2002 level.

The Olduwar People Group

Olduwar is a pseudonym we are giving to a predominantly Hindu people group in South Asia numbering just over one million. The Olduwar were the original inhabitants of a mountainous South Asian country that will remain unnamed.

Around 2002 the IMB assigned a missionary Strategy Coordinator to the Olduwar people. Over the following years, along with language study, the Strategy Coordinator began training whatever Christians he could find in reproducing evangelism and discipleship. As he did so, he cast a vision for reaching all the Olduwar people with the gospel. One of those who participated in the Coordinator's training was the senior pastor of a local network of churches called The Koinonia Network.

By 2006 the Strategy Coordinator reported a growing number of Olduwar believers attending his training events. These Olduwar believers spoke of increasing numbers of new Olduwar Christians and churches. Visitors to the region related that while walking through the crowded quarters of the capital city at night they could hear Christian songs in the Olduwar language wafting out to the streets below.

Eager to learn more, in May 2007 the IMB's regional leadership formed a team of South Asia missionaries to assess the status of gospel advance among the Olduwar. The team consisted of veteran missionaries who worked in a neighboring country. They began their survey with research drawn from published sources, other evangelical informants working in the country, and the annual statistical reports produced by the IMB's missionary to the Olduwar.

Surprising Turn in the Olduwar Movement

The assessment team traveled widely and conducted interviews in both urban and rural settings. They interviewed a range of Olduwar believers as well as anyone they could find who worked among the Olduwar. In the summer of 2007 the team produced a fifteen-page summary of their findings.

The Olduwar survey estimated that between seven thousand and ten thousand Olduwar Hindus had likely come to faith in Jesus Christ over the preceding decade. However, the assessment also noted that very few house churches existed among the Olduwar. Instead, the new Olduwar believers had been assimilated into the vibrant Koinonia Network of growing megachurches.

This was the same Koinonia Network whose senior pastor had participated in some of the early training sessions led by the IMB's Strategy Coordinator. The pastor had, in fact, adapted many portions of the training into his own church-growth plan. In the years that followed, the Koinonia Network had become the primary recipients of the substantial turning of Olduwar to Christ.

The assessment teams' findings were unexpected. While their survey did not invalidate the missionary's reports of burgeoning numbers of Olduwar believers, it revealed a surprising turn of direction. Perhaps due to the missionary's lack of emphasis in his strategy on planting house churches, a different model of church filled the gap, as most of the new Olduwar believers were now members of megachurches in the Koinonia Network.

The team discovered that the Koinonia Network consisted of

thirty-nine large churches ranging in size from a few hundred to three thousand members. While the Koinonia churches had seen considerable new fruit among the Olduwar, it was no Church Planting Movement. Nevertheless, the team found evidence that the Koinonia pastor had incorporated many lessons from the Strategy Coordinator's training. The Network's members held daily prayer meetings and had taken responsibility for evangelizing their community. And, despite their large congregations, they had also formed three hundred home fellowships to better disciple their growing numbers.

The assessment team's survey of the Olduwar movement validated the missionary's evangelism training but also revealed deficits in his strategy. In their final report the assessment team rejoiced that the Koinonia churches were vibrant and healthy, even though they were not the sort of lay-led house churches the team had anticipated.

Assessing Nine Subsa People Groups

We will conclude this chapter with nine assessments in an African country we will call Subsa. Subsa was one of many African nations located in the Sahel region. The *Sahel*, which means "shoreline" in Arabic, stretches 3,400 miles from West Africa to the Red Sea. Despite its name, the Sahel is not the shore of any body of water. It is, instead, the southern shore of the Sahara Desert, a vast ocean of sand that is also the ideological battleground between expanding Islam in the north and growing Christianity in the south.

Because the Sahel remains highly conflicted, we will use pseudonyms for the agency and people groups depicted below. Nonetheless, each of the cases described below come directly from the IMB's January 2017 report and the statistical reports provided by the sponsoring mission agency that we will call MovementCatalysts.

In the early 2000s MovementCatalysts invited one of the IMB's former Strategy Coordinators to join their staff to expand their church planting efforts on the international arena. As MovementCatalysts' reach extended into the broader world, they developed partnerships with like-minded, non-Western mission leaders who deployed Strategy Coordinators to unreached people groups in their region. The primary role of MovementCatalysts was to provide training and strategic resources to these Strategy Coordinators with the aim of catalyzing new Church Planting Movements. Within a few years MovementCatalysts had a growing network of indigenous partners around the world who were pursuing Church Planting Movements.

Much of the work of these local Strategy Coordinators was in hostile settings where missionary activity was under pressure from government and societal opposition. As MovementCatalysts navigated these new frontiers, they were reliant upon the reports that filtered up from the field to determine progress. In 2005 MovementCatalysts conducted their first international field report, which covered four African regions. They published a second survey in 2012 that tracked their progress from 2005.

Being aware of the potential for confirmation bias, MovementCatalysts sought an external assessment to evaluate their growing ministry. In 2016 they reached out to the International Mission Board for assistance. The IMB's director of Global Research agreed to help.

In April 2016 Dr. Jim Haney and Rita Salter led an assessment of nine different ethnolinguistic people groups in Subsa. Haney had spent years as a missionary in Africa and knew the terrain well. Salter, who served as the IMB's Sub-Saharan Africa Engagement Research Team Leader, played a crucial role in interviewing women. Haney and Salter were joined by two observers from MovementCatalysts, along with African partners Hussein, Robinson, and Jones.[2]

In 2016 Subsa had a rapidly growing, multiethnic population of several million inhabitants. Preliminary research revealed that Subsa was one of the poorest countries in the world, with 90 percent of its citizens living on less than six US dollars per day. Life-threatening diseases were endemic, and life expectancy was less than fifty-eight years. Two-thirds of the population was nonliterate, and civil wars had depleted the country's already limited resources.

Islam was Subsa's majority faith with Protestant Christianity scattered among several of their ethnolinguistic communities. Despite these two major religions, African Traditional Religions (ATRs) persisted widely and continued to influence both Christian and Muslim practices at a popular level.

The survey team determined it would not be feasible to travel into all the regions of Subsa to gather testimonies. The presence of white outsiders could skew the results and pose genuine hardships for the informants. Instead, the team conducted their interviews in two centralized locations, transporting informants to these venues from their remote homelands within the country.

Bussing Subsa informants into central locations meant true random samplings were not really an option. Thus, their projected numbers were drawn from the information provided by the limited number of informants who arrived for interviews. The team asked these informants a range of questions related to CPMs/DMMs, including whether or not the informants detected evidence of a movement, and captured their answers under the headings *Abundant, Some,* and *Little to None.*

---

2. These names are redacted for security purposes.

The Walu

The Walu were an agricultural people numbering about 25,000 with a larger population in a neighboring country. African Traditional Religion was widespread among the Walu beneath a veneer of Islam, which claimed about 90 percent of the population. There were also small numbers of Catholic, Methodist, and Pentecostal Walu churches. Nonetheless, in terms of Christian ministry, the team found the Walu to be among the most neglected people groups in the country.

On April 4 the assessment team began their survey with eleven Walu informants, four of whom were pastors, and two of whom were women. The informants related that dreams, good and bad, had contributed to their turning to Christianity, and they testified to spiritual power encounters that characterized the front lines of gospel advance.

The Walu informants spoke of praying for their neighbors as a prelude to sharing their faith with them. As an entry strategy for reaching their community, one of the Walu churches had started a school. Nevertheless, the informants said that new believers were often persecuted by members of the local mosques. They also faced opposition from Walu secret societies that practiced occultic African Traditional Religions.

The team discovered that some internal obstacles hindered the growth potential among the Walu. Rather than lay-led house churches, the Walu Christians were dependent upon pastors for leading the churches. The Walu pastors' insistence upon six months of discipleship before administering baptism was intended to strengthen the doctrinal foundation of the church's growth, but it also impeded rapid multiplication.

From their interviews the team estimated the existence of 24 Walu churches with 500 members. This was considerably less than the 2012 MovementCatalysts' report of 211 churches with 3,683 total disciples. As a result, both the informants and survey team agreed that a movement was not yet underway among the Walu.

The Sobay

On the same day, April 4, eleven informants arrived from the Sobay region of the country. The informants represented six different Sobay churches. The team noted that three of the informants were pastors and four were women.

The Sobay were an agricultural people with a population of about 200,000 that spilled over into Subsa from their larger population of 2.5 million living in a neighboring country. The Sobay population was more than 90 percent Sunni Muslim.

The informants were almost entirely from an Islamic background. They spoke of using a school as an evangelistic outreach to the community. Their ministry was characterized by prayer and the use of Discovery Bible Studies to evangelize and disciple.

Unlike the Walu, the Sobay pastors encouraged their members to baptize those they led to Christ. Nonetheless, the informants knew of only six churches among the Sobay with no more than fifteen Sobay Christians in those churches. These numbers contrasted sharply with MovementCatalysts' 2012 report of 235 churches with 8,930 members. As a result of the still-modest size of the Sobay work, the assessment team determined the work was still in its infancy.

The Anko

On April 5 the team interviewed eleven informants from the Anko people. Four of the informants were pastors, two were the African missionaries to the Anko, and one was an Anko woman.

The Anko resided in the mountains of Subsa where they subsisted as farmers. African Traditional Religion was predominant among them with a sizable Muslim population as well. According to Joshua Project research, about 3 percent of the Anko were Christian, though not evangelicals.

The informants reported using prayer and a new school start as evangelistic outreach to their community. They bemoaned the existence of persecution, stating, "If we start a church in our home, the Muslim landlord will evict us."

The team was impressed by the informants' stories of how nonliterate women were using prayer and evangelism to start new churches. When asked how they led Bible studies without literacy, they said they used "The Proclaimer," an audio Bible to communicate the gospel.

From the informants the team estimated the existence of 32 Anko churches with 480 members. This number was significantly less than the 159 churches with 4,293 Anko believers reported to MovementCatalysts in 2012. Given this revised number, both the informants and the assessment team agreed that a movement had yet to break among the Anko people.

The Yani

Also on April 5, the assessment team received eleven Christian informants from the Yani people. One of the informants was a pastor, and four were women. At the time of the assessment, the Yani had a total population of about 200,000, mostly Islamic adherents. About 50,000 Yani lived in Subsa, with the remaining 150,000 residing in neighboring countries.

The Yani Christians spoke of using Discovery Bible Studies in their churches and were deeply committed to prayer. The average Yani church membership, the team learned, was twenty to twenty-five members, typically not meeting in homes, but in dedicated church buildings. The Yani converts faced considerable persecution from the Imams in the village mosques. When asked, four of the Yani informants reported "Abundant" CPM strategy, but "Little or No" evidence of CPMs existing now. The other seven replied "Some" to both questions.

Based on the informants' testimonies, the assessment team estimated a likely total of 69 Yani churches with 1,725 baptized members. These numbers compared favorably with the 71 churches and 833 baptized disciples reported in MovementCatalysts' 2012 statistical report. The growth attested to the informants' testimonies of abundant gospel sowing.

Informants revealed that the work suffered from leadership deficits and dependence upon dedicated church buildings, which the impoverished and persecuted minority was unable to establish. While the Yani work showed promise, the team concluded it had not yet reached a tipping point to become a Church Planting Movement. For a movement to take place, the team recommended that the Yani Christians decentralize into house churches and receive training to empower local leaders to take ownership of the movement.

The Koro

On April 6 the team conducted an assessment of the Koro people. The Koro resided primarily in the southeastern region of Subsa where there were as many as sixteen different Christian denominations at work. Four of the eleven Koro informants were women, and one was their pastor who had come to Christ from a Muslim background. Though Joshua Project research indicated that the Koro were mostly adherents to African Traditional Religions, with up to 14 percent evangelical population, most of the informants said they lived in an Islamic context.

The Koro Christians stated that 65 percent of their people had little or no access to churches. They were also concerned that their language was becoming extinct. Even the Koro pastor confided that he could not speak the Koro language, preaching instead through an interpreter. They further stated that perhaps

20 percent of their churches had been lost to an Ebola outbreak. They lamented that both Muslims and Catholics persecuted the new Koro Christians. Despite these hardships, the team observed that each of the Koro informants expressed great joy in their faith.

From the interviews, the team estimated the likely existence of 100 Koro churches with some 3,320 having been baptized. This number had risen considerably from the 40 churches with 600 members reported in 2012. While this growth showed that a CPM might be emerging among the Koro, it had not yet reached a tipping point. Consequently, the team felt the Koro ministry was not yet a Church Planting Movement, and the eleven Koro informants agreed.

The Fan

On April 7 and 8 the team interviewed seventeen Fan Christian informants, of whom two were pastors and three were women.

The Fan people were largely pastoralist and had a long history of Islam. Their population of 300,000 was 98 to 99 percent Muslim. As a result, each of the informants spoke of widespread persecution of any Fan who became a Christian. Nonetheless, they expressed strong faith and resilience.

The Fan Christians relied heavily upon prayer and Scripture. Those who could read often carried their Bibles with them when they traveled. Apostasy from Christianity was unknown to the informants, though there was some evidence of syncretism that strayed from biblical norms. Dreams about Jesus and answered prayers for healing were some of the major ways that Fan people were coming to Christ.

Haney described one of the Fan informants as a "super-spreader" of the gospel. He defined a super-spreader as one who is "always ready to share and shares without fear." Haney noted that movements are built on super-spreaders.

It was striking that the assessment team was unable or unwilling to venture an estimate for the total number of Fan Christians or churches. This was unique among the nine Subsa people groups they surveyed. In MovementCatalysts' 2012 report, the Fan were said to have 145 churches with 4,060 baptized disciples. The 2016 survey team neither affirmed nor denied this number. Nonetheless, both the Fan informants and the assessors felt the Fan had not yet realized a movement of new disciples and churches.

The Daimu

On April 8 the assessment team conducted its survey of a pastoral people that we will call the Daimu. A 99 percent Islamic people group, the Daimu are found in the northern and eastern portions of Subsa and numbered 350,000 at the time of the survey. The team interviewed twelve informants from the Daimu people, four of whom were women.

The team quickly discovered that the African Strategy Coordinator to the Daimu people did not know the extent of the people group, nor was he in touch with the Daimu church leaders. This made it difficult for the team to determine the nature of the work.

Despite significant persecution from the Muslim majority, the Daimu Christians were passionate in their faith and shared the gospel widely. Several informants spoke of the role that dreams and miraculous healings had played in their conversion to Christ. They used soccer as an access strategy in Daimu villages and engaged Daimu Muslims with dialogue and prayer to share the gospel.

The team was surprised to learn that nonliterate Daimu women were active and effective in starting new churches. These women relied heavily on prayer and used the oral Bible transmitter called "The Proclaimer" to conduct Discovery Bible Studies as they traveled through Daimu villages. Their churches met wherever they could, even under trees.

Based upon these informant testimonies, the team estimated forty-five churches with 1,730 baptized believers among the Daimu. However, the numbers assessed were considerably less than MovementCatalysts' 2012 report of 239 churches with 8,843 disciples. The revised downward trajectory of the Daimu work indicated that a movement was not yet underway.

The Brosh

On April 9 the assessment team conducted interviews of eleven Brosh Christians, of whom one was a pastor and four were women.

The 130,000 Brosh people resided in the southern part of Subsa. The team's pre-field research had already determined that the Brosh people were likely not an unreached people group; 8 percent professed Christianity as their religion. However, the Brosh would certainly qualify as under-engaged, and their language was classified as endangered. At the time of the assessment, the Brosh had no Bible in their own language, which was exclusively oral. The Brosh were predominantly followers of African Traditional Religions. As the team probed issues of syncretism, the informants indicated that a third of the Brosh Christians continued to participate in the secret societies that were infused with the rituals of African Traditional Religion.

In their recommendations the team counseled the African Strategy Coordinator to incorporate orality methods such as storying, the Proclaimer, or even micro-SD cards in cell phones to provide the Brosh with access to Scripture in their own language.

Despite the challenges posed by the Brosh context, the team determined that evangelism and church planting among them was vibrant. The team estimated the existence of about 200 churches among the Brosh with as many as 10,000 baptized members, indicating significant Christian vitality among the Brosh. However, the 2016 estimates were down from the 336 churches with 19,152 members found in the 2012 report, belying the likelihood of a Church Planting Movement.

The Kusho

On April 9 the team conducted an assessment of the work among the Kusho people. The 68,000 Kusho resided in northeastern Subsa at the time of the survey. The team interviewed ten Kusho Christians, of whom three were pastors and two were women.

Once again, pre-field research indicated the Kusho were not an unreached people group. Though they were predominantly followers of African Traditional Religion, as much as 16 percent of their population identified themselves as evangelicals. Joshua Project research on the Kusho indicated an indeterminate Muslim population, yet the African missionary partner estimated that 20 percent of the Kusho were Muslim.

The assessment team learned that the African missionary assigned to the Kusho had not yet learned their language, and they recommended this should be his next priority. At the same time, the team found that the Kusho Christians themselves were natural evangelists who were using the Discovery Bible Studies method to great effect.

From their survey of the informants, the team estimated there were approximately 160 Kusho churches with roughly 8,500 baptized members. This number was not as high as the 194 churches with 10,864 discipled members reported in 2012. Accordingly, the team concluded that the work among the Kusho, though substantial, was probably not yet a Church Planting Movement. While each of the informants indicated "some" evidence of a movement, they generally concurred with the survey team's conclusions.

Yes, There Were Also Non-Movements

Debrief, Report, and Response

After a debriefing to review their notes, the team completed the field portion of their assessment. The team leader gathered the surveys and returned home to compile his report.

On January 24, 2017 Jim Haney shared his 140-page report with the leadership of MovementCatalysts. For each of the nine ministries, the team had recorded testimonies, summarized findings, and offered recommendations. The report provided valuable insights into what was occurring among each of these nine Subsa groups. In most instances they found that Christianity was indeed on the rise among these Muslim, nominal Christian, and African Traditional Religionists. At the same time, in each case, the team determined that growth had not yet reached Church Planting Movement or Disciple Making Movement levels, and their informants agreed.

This raises the question: What do you do when the first nine movements that your organization submits for external assessment prove to be less than movements? For a healthy organization, like MovementCatalysts, the answer was clear: celebrate the findings. These assessments provided a firm foundation for future ministry efforts.

In some instances MovementCatalysts may not have agreed with the conclusions made in the IMB's report, but they appreciated and affirmed the value of external assessments to better understand what God was doing in their ministry. They viewed the IMB's assessment, like their own regular evaluations done by local teams, as critical to providing opportunities for improvement. Even when the insights and recommendations weren't what they wanted to hear, they acknowledged that every ministry has areas of drift that need correction as well as indications of progress that deserve to be celebrated.

By 2024 MovementCatalysts' field assessments had evolved beyond simply recording numbers into a more robust assessment of the health of each local ministry. Their new tracking metrics examined quality as well as growth and multiplication. Today, MovementCatalysts' partnerships have spread into ninety-nine countries—where local Strategy Coordinators report quarterly on fourteen data points—measuring health, growth, and reproduction across multiple people-group engagements.

Concluding Comments

What can we say about these assessments that failed to identify Church Planting Movements? Were they failures? No. The assessments did their job, even when they disproved a negative. They were able to uncover deceptions, unexpected redirections, exaggerated realities, and even vibrant works whose potential as Church Planting Movements still awaited them.

Each of the missional entities that invited assessments was working toward Church Planting Movements. But good assessments do more than confirm biases. They hold up a mirror to what is actually happening—the good, the bad, and the ugly. The result is a better understanding of where God is working, where the missionary's strategy needs to be adjusted, and how the ministry can best proceed toward the goal of multiplying new disciples and churches.

As Church Planting Movements entered their third decade, missionaries were gaining new appreciation for assessments. They were learning that good assessments were invaluable to shaping effective strategy.

In the next chapter we will return to Africa where an ancient Islamic people were turning to Christ in remarkable numbers.

Yes, There Were Also Non-Movements

We'll then examine a CPM diaspora assessment that chased a movement across several countries. And, finally, we will see how a South Asian movement started 14,190 new churches in a single year.

NINE

MUSLIM, DIASPORA, AND HINDU MOVEMENTS

Despite the existence of non-movements, new Church Planting Movements and emerging movements continued to appear in the reports of both the International Mission Board missionaries and those of other agencies. As we have seen, though, the IMB's assessment teams were also evolving in their ability to discern the reality behind the reports.

While assessments were not always possible, the IMB's Global Research Team demonstrated considerable creativity and persistence in their efforts to examine the nature and scope of the ministries reported by their missionaries.

Back to Africa

The Foro people are the name we are giving to a family of linguistically related people groups that number more than twenty million and are scattered across eighteen countries from West

Africa to Ethiopia. Predominantly Islamic, these people display a range of lifestyles from nomadic to sedentary. The largest population of Foro resides in a West African country with a large and well-established Baptist denomination that had shown little interest in reaching their fourteeen million Foro compatriots.

The IMB missionary working among the Foro group was an unmarried woman whom we will call Mary. In addition to working at the local Baptist seminary, Mary had devoted more than a decade of ministry to the Foro. By the mid-2000s, Mary began to observe growing numbers of new believers and churches among the Foro. Her reports indicated that the work had grown from four churches in the late 1990s to more than three thousand believers by 2008.

Persecution among the new Foro believers was widespread, and Mary was not exempted from it. She had already seen the attacks firsthand when a violent mob of Muslim men stormed the Baptist seminary, shouting, "Find the white woman!"

By the grace of God, Mary eluded capture, but it was in this challenging context that she reached out to her regional leadership for guidance.

The Foro Assessment

In 2007 the IMB's West Africa regional leader turned to the Global Research Department for an in-depth analysis. That same year Jim Slack began compiling data on the Foro in preparation for an onsite assessment. His research began with the history of Baptist work in the country dating back to the 1850s, which provided him with valuable context for the new initiatives and reports submitted by Mary.

The assessment team's report reflected a comprehensive effort to gather data from a variety of sources. These included the work of other agencies such as SIM (Serving for International Missions), New Life for All, the Lutheran Church, the Christian Reformed Church, the Churches of Christ, the Evangelical Church in West Africa, Wycliffe Bible Translators, and several gospel radio broadcasts in the Foro language. Additionally, the team benefited from a PhD dissertation published in 2000 by Mogens Stensbeck at Fuller Theological Seminary. Stensbeck's examination of multiagency efforts to reach the Foro had identified as many as 825 baptized Foro believers related to five different mission agencies.

The CPM assessment team concentrated their efforts in two overwhelmingly Islamic states with a history of violence against Christians. Mary had spent many years living and working in these two states, and it was here that she identified the epicenter of the purported movement. The team brought with them the 121-question survey instrument they had refined over previous years.

The team arrived on the field in January 2008 to conduct their onsite survey. For security reasons the report doesn't state the team members' names, but indicates there were persons on the team who knew languages related to the Foro language, as well as one person who had been a New Tribes translator, mentor, and worldview specialist in Southeast Asia.

Since it was not safe for outsiders to wander into Muslim Foro villages and ask questions, the assessment team came up with a creative solution. Mary informed them of a Bible conference in which Foro Christian leaders and believers were gathering for teaching and training. During the conference the assessment team pulled aside individuals and small groups for interviews.

The team's goal was to randomly interview at least seventy-five to one hundred believers and leaders among the Foro Christians. Ultimately ninety-five respondents participated, and each of the interviews took from one to three hours. From these interviews, Slack was able to cross-reference the data to determine the nature of the conversions, styles of worship, leadership and leadership training patterns, ages and gender of those being reached, and frequency of persecution, among other factors.

Though the informants were not randomly selected from the total Foro population, the team carefully tracked data on each of the persons they interviewed. They asked their age, gender, when they first heard the gospel, when they made a decision to follow Christ, if and when they were baptized, the location and size of their church, whether they had led others to Christ, and if so, how?

From their research and informant interviews, the assessment team concluded that indeed a Church Planting Movement was underway among the Foro. The number of churches had grown from 85 in 2003 to 390 in 2008, while the total number of Foro believers had grown from 1,200 in 2003 to approximately 4,952 in 2008. The team concluded that Mary had actually underreported the size of the movement by 65 percent.

The team was surprised that the growth in the work among the Foro had largely escaped detection by the national Baptist denomination that had thrived in the country for more than a century. The reasons for this oversight soon became apparent.

The membership of the Baptist denomination was almost entirely comprised of ethnic communities with no Islamic background. Only recently had the Baptist churches begun to give attention to the nearly 50 percent of their nation who identified as Muslims. The assessment team discovered that the national Baptist denomination had relegated one- to two hundred of the Foro churches reported by the missionary to be "outreach groups," as they did not meet the denomination's institutional definition of a church. However, the assessment team found that these one- to two hundred groups functioned fully as churches and counted them as such.

The team also investigated the ways that new churches were being started in this hostile environment. They were particularly sensitive to the role that foreign subsidies often played in church planting. Their findings concluded that

> there is no issue of subsidy needed ... to reproduce (churches) or in the paying of pastors. .... What subsidy comments they talked about were related to meeting medical needs, seeking pure water, gaining what schooling a nomadic life allowed, and especially attending the annual conferences.

Regarding the issue of syncretism, when the team asked informants directly, 88.5 percent of them confirmed they had made a deliberate choice to break with the Islamic religion when they embraced Jesus as Lord.

In January 2009 the assessment team produced a seventy-seven-page confidential report with a wealth of detailed information. On June 18, 2009 Slack circulated his confidential report to the team members and then to the West Africa regional office in January 2010. The assessment team's report included seven recommendations and nine sub-recommendations to the mission for strategic enhancement moving forward.

An Islamic Diaspora Movement

Shistan is the name we are giving to an Islamic Middle Eastern country where persecution of Christianity is widespread and sanctioned by the government. By 2010 rumors of growing Christianity in Shistan had become a broad topic of speculation across the evangelical world. However, the closed political conditions in Shistan left outsiders to speculate and, at times, exaggerate the state of Christianity in the country.

The IMB had not fielded missionaries in Shistan since an Islamic revolution in the 1970s had resulted in the expulsion of all foreign missionaries. In the decades that followed, however, the nation's citizens themselves began to exit their homeland and soon began appearing in neighboring countries and Western European cities. By 2021 more than four million emigrants from Shistan had scattered around the globe. Missionaries, including IMB teams, followed these diaspora communities with ministry and gospel witness. Those working among the Shistan diaspora attested to the remarkable openness to the gospel exhibited by these Muslim refugees.

By 2010, both IMB missionaries and the broader evangelical community were reporting that refugees from Shistan were perhaps the most responsive Muslims in the world to the gospel. They further speculated that Muslims from Shistan just might represent the greatest turning to Christ in the Muslim world. Reports from radio and satellite television broadcasts, Internet evangelism, and the assimilation of Bibles into Shistan and their diaspora communities all lent credence to the speculation.

By 2011 IMB missionaries working with the Shistan diaspora sought help in evaluating the scope and health of the burgeoning movement. In 2013 the IMB's Global Research Department began preparations for their most ambitious assessment—measuring a movement that was dispersed around the world.[1]

Assessing a Diaspora Movement

Assessing an Islamic diaspora people group posed new challenges; and though costly in time and resources, the assessment teams rose to the occasion.[2] The Islamic diaspora under review

---

1. Personal testimonies from this movement are recorded in David Garrison, *A Wind in the House of Islam* (Monument, CO: WIGTake Resources, 2014).

2. Among the challenges was the cost of deploying assessment teams to multiple countries to inspect the fruit of a movement that was scattered globally.

Muslim, Diaspora, and Hindu Movements

were exclusively emigrants from Shistan who had gone through a harsh, anti-Christian Islamic revolution resulting in the expulsion of missionaries and emigration of millions of citizens from the country.

Both the emigrants and efforts to reach them extended far beyond the work of the International Mission Board. Nonetheless, in four phases IMB assessment teams were able to visit Shistani diaspora communities, and they discovered sizable numbers of new believers among them in seven countries. This confirmed the existence of multiple Church Planting Movements among the diaspora as well as in the homeland from which they had emigrated.

Between January 27 and February 8, 2012, the first phase of the IMB assessment commenced. The team consisted of Dr. Jim Slack, with veteran missionaries to Muslims Dr. David Garrison, Dr. Jon Gresham, and IMB staff researcher Scott Peterson, accompanied by four Muslim-background Christian translators from Shistan.

Phase One took place in an Islamic country neighboring Shistan that had received several million Shistan emigrants. Some of these emigrants were transiting to other lands while others were making the adjacent country their new home. Phase One surveyed a variety of ethnolinguistic communities who had fled from Shistan and settled in eleven different cities in the neighboring country. Over twelve days the team conducted interviews with 130 informants, listening to their stories and compiling data in an Excel spreadsheet with 99 datapoints.[3]

Then, between July 2 and July 15, 2013 a Phase Two team composed of Slack, Peterson, and IMB Shistani-speaking missionaries A. and J. Boyd surveyed fourteen different Shistan

---

3. Some of the informant stories from the Phase One survey are incorporated into Garrison, *A Wind in the House of Islam*.

diaspora communities in Holland, Belgium, and the United Kingdom. The Boyds followed this survey with Phase Three, from July 17 to 22, by examining ministries to the Shistani diaspora in Germany and Greece. Finally, Phase Four was conducted the same year with surveys of Shistani emigrants by missionaries Jim S. and Sally H. in Houston, Texas.[4]

In September 2014 Jim Slack issued a fifty-seven-page confidential report on the status of movements among the Shistani diaspora. Despite the breadth of the survey, the final report was modest in its conclusions: "While the number of interviews is insufficient to establish with confidence the quantitative size of a CPM among the Shistani diaspora, we believe that interviews provide sufficient support for a number of CPMs that have emerged and are continuing to emerge."

Notably, the report stated, "Today, it is no exaggeration to say that the only thing growing faster than Christianity in Shistan is the wave of disaffected apostates abandoning Islam." Surprisingly, Slack's final report made no reference to the 130 interviews that had been conducted in the Phase One survey. Instead, he drew the bulk of his conclusions from the second-, third- and fourth-phase interviews gathered from diaspora Shistani living in the five Western European countries and the U.S.; no explanation was given for this decision. However, as a member of the Phase One survey, I can report that multiple Shistani house churches were detected in the country neighboring Shistan and were scattered across each of the eleven cities visited.

The final assessment report was revealing. The survey estimated there were approximately 250 Shistani evangelical believers living in Belgium; 800 in Holland; as many as 3,000 in the United Kingdom; about 500 in Germany; and a further 200 Shistani believers in Greece.

---

4. Team member names have been redacted for security purposes.

Though movements to Christ were widespread among the Shistani diaspora, many informants pointed back to their homeland as the center of the growing work. The report concluded that "there is a rapid multiplication of indigenous churches within Shistan, and this movement has moved into streams in the diaspora." The survey pointed out that Shistan is a multi-ethnic nation, and there appeared to be movements to Christ in many, if not most, of Shistan's varied ethnicities.

Combining the number of evangelicals in Shistan with twenty nations containing sizable diaspora populations the team estimated a total of 99,385 Shistani Christians. Of these, 87,161 were still living inside Shistan. The survey teams determined that these new Shistani Muslim-background Christians were worshipping in approximately 642 faith communities that were taking root all over the world.

A Quellestan Movement in South Asia

Quellestan is the name we are giving to a predominantly Hindu state in South Asia with a population of approximately 70 million. In December 2005 a young IMB couple was deployed to a city in Quellestan. The couple's first few years on the field were spent learning the language, understanding the culture, and growing their family. It was also a season of ministry frustration.

Disappointed by the lack of response from their people group, the couple experimented with several evangelistic approaches before settling on orality-based communication of the gospel through a method that they called "Creation to New Creation (C2NC)." C2NC consisted of thirty-five Bible stories that included "a 5-part CPM process designed to grow a person that had never heard the name of Jesus into a self-feeding disciple maker."

By 2012 the couple began to see breakthroughs as Quellestani partners went through their training and joined their work. The work was further accelerated with the introduction of micro-SD cards containing both the C2NC training material and the entire Bible in audio format. This technology allowed the largely non-literate people of Quellestan to listen to the lessons and Scripture through their own ubiquitous smartphones. By 2018 the couple was reporting a total of more than 19,000 churches planted across the state. Then, in 2020, the couple counted 14,190 new churches planted in the previous year.

Before delving into these reports let's take a closer look at Quellestan. Quellestan's population was overwhelmingly Hindu at 88 percent, of whom more than six million were high-caste Brahmins. The state also had a sizable Muslim population of more than six million. With more than twenty million low-caste citizens, Quellestan had one of the highest illiteracy rates in South Asia. Most citizens of Quellestan were agriculturalists, many of whom were day laborers and sharecroppers.

The remarkable church growth reports from Quellestan did not escape the attention of the International Mission Board home office. Even before the IMB couple submitted their stunning 2020 annual report claiming 14,190 new church starts the previous year, eyebrows were raising on the home front. As reports of the couple's work filtered up to IMB trustees in the spring of 2020, board members felt compelled to request both a qualitative and quantitative audit of the work in Quellestan.

The Quellestan Assessment

By 2020 the work in Quellestan had been buttressed by nearly fifteen years of monthly reports to their field supervisor and annual statistical reports to the IMB's Global Research Department. However, any report claiming 14,190 new churches in a single

Muslim, Diaspora, and Hindu Movements

year was bound to draw attention from vigilant trustees whose vantage points were much less prolific American churches.

In one of their spring 2020 meetings, the IMB trustees requested an official assessment of the Quellestani work. The Global Research Department, then headed by veteran South Asia and Middle East missionary Wilson Geisler, began their pre-field preparation.

In addition to constructing a research profile of Quellestan, Geisler elevated his survey to a new level. By the time of the 2020 assessment, the Global Research Department had received over 14,000 pages of reports on the growth of the work. Geisler's team submitted the data regarding each of the 14,190 new churches reported in 2020 to the website Random.org. The online randomizer told Geisler how many churches and informants would be required to gain a 90 percent confidence level with a 5 percent margin of error. The program then used an algorithm to select which churches should be surveyed to gain an accurate sampling. The algorithm determined that the team would need to collect interviews from 270 randomly selected churches.

Then, in March 2020 with assistance from the South Asia regional leadership, a team of fourteen veteran missionaries converged on Quellestan to begin a survey. In consultation with the regional field director, Geisler chose assessment team members from missionaries who were not a part of the Quellestan ministry, each of whom had achieved a high-level of language competency in the national language spoken in Quellestan. Nonetheless, local translators were used to penetrate the various heart languages spoken in the state. Added to the nuance of the assessment effort, the IMB's chairman of the board appointed four trustees to oversee the assessment process.

By the end of the three-week onsite assessment, the team had managed to interview only 240 of the desired 270 churches—89 percent of the target number. The shortfall was attributed to the fact that many church members were agricultural laborers and were away from home working in the fields. Undeterred, the team added an additional 114 churches they knew to be more mature, meaning three to five years old, for a total assessment of 384 churches. The team hoped that by surveying 114 older churches they could determine if any of the older churches had ceased to exist or had strayed from their evangelical roots.

The assessment team used a survey instrument with forty-eight questions and thirty sub-questions that varied little from those that had been pioneered by Jim Slack two decades earlier. Their Quellestan survey instrument is included in Appendix C at the end of this book.

The team was tasked with evaluating both the quality and size of the work. They discovered qualitatively that the values the missionary couple had emphasized were now being reflected throughout the churches themselves. These key distinctives were (1) prayer, (2) every member ministry, (3) tracking at every level, and (4) focus on households for evangelism and church formation.

Though the new believers in the Quellestan movement were largely nonliterate, the missionary's provision of audio Bibles had resulted in Bible saturation among the new believers. More than 70 percent of those surveyed spoke of daily engagement with Scripture. A further 79 percent of the informants reported having discipled someone themselves. An additional 75 percent of those surveyed were able to quote some portion of Scripture.

Quantitatively, the assessment determined that some churches had multiplied to the twentieth generation since beginning in 2012. The team determined that only one of the 14,190 new churches started in 2019 no longer met. However, they also concluded that 31 percent of the churches no longer fully met the IMB's rigorous definition of church, despite meeting multiple times each week in small groups. In some instances smaller groups had merged together into larger networks due to the local believers' desire to share the Lord's Supper in a larger community or share leadership over several house groups.

From the team's survey of 114 "more mature," three- to five-year-old churches, they found that 100 percent were still active as churches. Of these, 88.6 percent had identifiable leaders, 91 percent practiced baptism, 85 percent took the Lord's Supper, 94 percent were involved in discipleship, 74 percent gave tithes and offerings, 99 percent engaged in regular worship, and 96 percent received regular teaching or preaching.

The Quellestan survey was the most recent in a long line of CPM assessments, and it represented the most thorough assessment conducted to date. In May 2022 the Global Research Department and field leadership team filtered through the massive volume of data and generated a 35-page report to the IMB board of trustees. The 2022 annual statistical report for the Quellestan movement confirmed 40,694 churches with 121,847 baptized church members.

Upon the completion of the assessment, one of the trustee observers confessed to fellow board members with a smile: "Well, brethren, I've got bad news for you . . . *it's real.*" To the credit of the International Mission Board trustees, they had investigated for themselves and become convinced that Church Planting Movements, though beyond the scope of their personal ministry experience, were quite real.

Concluding Observations

By 2024, reports of new Church Planting Movements were emerging in many corners of the world's least-reached lands. Movements were not the norm, however, as most missionaries continued to struggle to reach their first converts, first disciples, and first churches. As they aspired to see indigenous, self-replicating churches, though, some of these works reached a tipping point and movements ensued.

Few assessments will ever have the luxury of randomly selecting 270 of 14,190 churches from which to determine the truth of what is taking place. Few mission agencies have the capacity of a Global Research Department that can launch teams in four phases across hundreds of miles and seven countries to track the movements of God across widely scattered diaspora populations. And, sadly, most Christians will never have the benefit of seeing a new movement firsthand.

For these reasons questions regarding movements may never cease, and the picture of what is happening may never be fully resolved. However, honest efforts to assess them are being undertaken, and with them, our knowledge of how God is at work in these movements is increasing.

In the next section we will turn our attention to the future. We will learn about new tools that are being developed and adapted to track the growth and nature of movements. We will also learn about new perspectives that show great promise in the understanding of how Church Planting Movements are unfolding.

PART THREE

THE ROAD AHEAD

TEN

NEW TOOLS AND PERSPECTIVES

As Church Planting Movements enter their third decade, we are acquiring new tools for assessing them, new perspectives for understanding them, and new methods for pursuing them.

New Measuring Tools

The earliest diagrams of church multiplication were scribbled out by missionaries on notebooks, whiteboards, and even sheets of cardboard. How else could one track a church that started another that started another, extending out for multiple generations? And, even when you did, how could a person account for the differences in each church—which were healthy, which were deficient, and what deficiencies needed to be addressed?

Today's missionaries have grown up with smartphones and laptop computers that employ icons rather than words to navigate their features. By the early 2000s South Asia missionaries

Nathan and Kari Shank began experimenting with icons to delineate new churches, their health, and their generations of reproduction.[1]

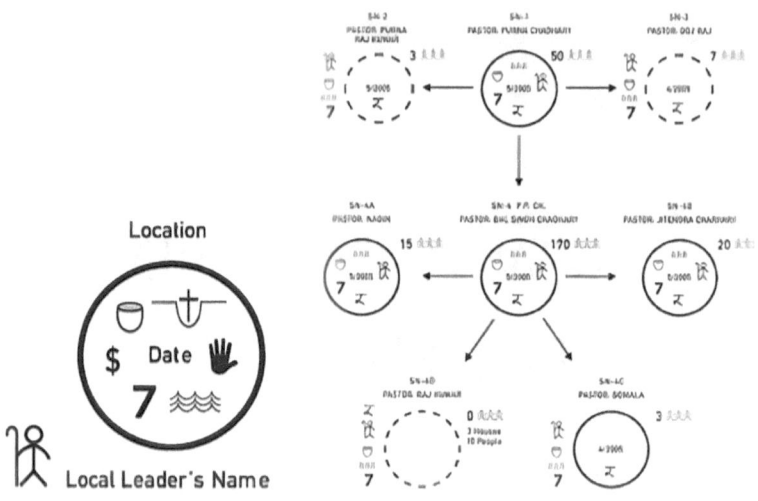

In 2018 Shank's colleagues in South Asia developed a smartphone app called "GenMapper" that missionaries used to locate and track new church plants using icons and satellite geolocation.[2] The smartphone tool not only allowed missionaries to pinpoint the exact location of churches—but also to measure key aspects of church health—such as baptism and the Lord's Supper, Bible teaching, evangelism, discipleship, leadership, and training.

Soon after, Assemblies of God missionaries working in the Middle East developed their own app-based tracking tool called

---

1. See Nathan Shank's "Generational Mapping: Tracking Elements of Church Formation Within CPMs," in *Mission Frontiers*, November 1, 2012. Though the article did not appear until 2012, Shank developed this in South Asia prior to 2009.

2. GenMapper refers to "generation mapper," a tool that tracks generations of churches planting churches. A ghost of the GenMapper app is still found on the Apple App Store, though its functions have now been expanded and absorbed into Ta Ethni's GAPP (Gospel to All Peoples and Places) app. See also, Nathan Shank, "Generational Mapping: Tracking Elements of Church Planting in Church Planting Movements" in *Mission Frontiers*, November 1, 2012.

"Pattern." The tool's designers described it as "a language independent application that facilitates the secure sharing of resources and empowerment of every believer as a disciple maker and church planter."[3] Since the Pattern app is customizable to include everything from Bible lessons to church organization, it circulated widely among missionaries working in restricted-access countries. Security was a primary concern for the app's developers, who took important steps to ensure data confidentiality.

In 2018 the Southern Baptist International Mission Board began collaboration with a company called *Ta Ethni* (The Nations) to develop a new cloud-based app called GAPP (Gospel to All Peoples and Places).

Like the GenMapper and Pattern apps before it, Ta Ethni's GAPP software used icons to map and assess healthy church formation, and track generational reproduction, while also recording key statistics such as evangelism, discipleship, and leadership development. A language translation feature enabled partners from virtually any language community to use the app. In addition to measuring the quality and quantity of churches, GAPP's mapping interface allowed church planters to identify ministry activities that contributed to new church starts anywhere in the world. With a priority concern for protecting the app's data, Ta Ethni annually tests the security of the program by hiring professional hackers to try to breach its firewall.

In February 2024, after more than a year of beta testing, Ta Ethni released GAPP to the broader evangelical world. By 2025 GAPP was being used by thousands of multiethnic missionaries and church planters.[4] GenMapper, Pattern, and GAPP are just a few of the tools that missionaries and the agencies that support them are using to track the quality and quantity of their work.

---

3. See the Pattern App Launch Center, https://patternlaunch.com/, accessed May 23, 2025.

4. See GAPP Usage Counter at https://taethni.com/gapp/, accessed March 30, 2025.

At this point, Church Planting Movement assessments have primarily focused on two aspects of their subject: quantity and quality. These dimensions of movements will remain at the forefront of CPM assessments for the foreseeable future. However, other perspectives into movements are beginning to surface. Let's turn our attention to some of the more promising new fields of CPM study.

Through a Physician's Lens

In 2008 Charles Fielding, the pen name of a missionary physician with decades of work among unreached peoples in South Asia, Africa, and the Middle East, brought his unique insights to Church Planting Movements. Fielding applied his medical perspective to the ten universal elements of a Church Planting Movement first described by this author in 1999.[5] He noticed they could be clustered into three distinct categories: Ingredients, Methods, and Products.

Fielding described *ingredients* as "what you do." To this category he assigned (1) prayer, (2) abundant gospel sowing, and (3) intentional church planting. Under *methods* or "how you do it," he identified four elements: (4) scriptural authority, (5) local leadership, (6) lay leadership, and (7) cell/house-church format. Finally, he defined *products* as "what will result." He identified these resulting outcomes as (8) churches planting churches, (9) rapid reproduction, and (10) healthy churches.

In short, Fielding saw that the right ingredients coupled with the right methods should generate predictable outcomes. He noted:

---

5. David Garrison, *Church Planting Movements* booklet, 1999.

If you took high-school chemistry, you can think of elements one through three as the ingredients that the apostolic teams added to the environment. Elements four through seven are the methods by which the apostolic ministers did their work. Elements eight through 10 are the products that resulted from the work. The apostolic ministers themselves were primarily catalysts, which sped up the process and precipitated the results.[6]

The Math of Movements

Chris Keener, a PhD in physics, and his colleague Dave Foster approached movements from a mathematical perspective. In their thought-provoking essay, published in the January 2025 issue of *Global Missiology*, the authors began with the acknowledgment that "Disciple Making Movements are . . . a movement of God. Without Him, there is nothing."[7] However, they also recognized the important roles played by missionaries and the communities they were trying to reach.

Keener and Foster identified three key components in movements as (1) the gospel communicators, (2) the recipients of the message, and (3) the relational connectivity of those gospel recipients.

Using these elements Keener and Foster constructed a mathematical model to analyze the movement process. They cross-referenced high and low gospel receptivity with high and low relational connectivity to identify four types of

---

6. Charles Fielding, MD, *Preach and Heal, a Biblical Model for Missions* (Richmond, VA: International Mission Board, SBC, 2008), ch. 5.

7. Chris Keener and Dave Foster, "A Mathematically Based Model of Disciple Making Movements," in *Global Missiology*, Vol. 22, no. 1, January 2025. Quote from Glenn Sunshine and Jerry Trousdale, *The Kingdom Unleashed* (Murfreesboro, TN: DMM Library, 2018).

communities. The resulting analysis suggested eleven different strategic approaches missionaries could take to optimize a Disciple Making Movement among their people group.

Keener and Foster's fresh look at movements provided missionaries with another useful tool for understanding their people group. It also offered valuable guidance for those who wanted to optimize their time and methods as they sought to catalyze a movement of new disciples.[8]

Sociocultural Explorations

Warrick Farah is the pen name used by an Arabic-speaking missionary with years of service in the Middle East. Over the past decade Farah has increasingly turned his attention to the study of Church Planting Movements.

In 2020 Farah hosted an online global gathering of missionary church planters, mission strategists, and academics to ask, "What is God doing in Church Planting Movements?" Students and practitioners of movements from Southeast Asia to Africa spent two days on their Zoom feeds to discuss CPM case studies.

The following year William Carey Publishing issued the contents of Farah's online forum in a book called *Motus Dei: The Movement of God to Disciple the Nations*.[9] The anthology examined the phenomenon of Church Planting Movements from an array of perspectives: theological, missiological, methodological, biblical, historical, and contemporary. Farah's book introduced the term "movements missiology" to the vocabulary of the mission community, providing an important contribution

---

8. Keener and Foster, "A Mathematically Based Model of Disciple Making Movements."

9. Warrick Farah, *Motus Dei: The Movement of God to Disciple the Nations* (Pasadena: William Carey Pub., 2021).

to the curricula of seminaries, Bible colleges, and theological institutions.

Academic Attention

To date, academic institutions have generated more criticism of Church Planting Movements than scholarly investigations into them. Some graduate seminary programs have even pressed their students to redefine Church Planting Movements into more familiar terms such as "revivals" or "harvests of new believers." These attempts to fit new phenomena into nineteenth-century paradigms and vocabulary reveal much about the academic lag in missiological studies.

Undeterred by hesitant seminaries, some missionaries have forced the issue. With personal experience of Church Planting Movements, these missionaries used their furloughs to pursue graduate studies, and they brought with them the subject of movements. In 2013 Overseas Missionary Fellowship (OMF) missionary Frank Schattner entered Biola University's Cook School of Intercultural Studies to explore how the Church Planting Movements he was seeing in East Asia could better balance scriptural grounding with vitality and sustainability.[10]

In 2014 Steve Smith wrote *An Evaluation of Training for Trainers (T4T) as an Aid for Developing Sustained Church Planting Movements (CPMs)* as his dissertation thesis at the University of South Africa.[11] Two years later Mary Ho, president of the pioneering agency All Nations in Kansas City, Missouri, sought to adapt

---

10. Frank Schattner. *Sustainability Within Church-Planting Movements in East Asia*, a dissertation presented to the faculty of the Cook School of Intercultural Studies at Biola University, May 2013.

11. Steve Smith, *An Evaluation of Training for Trainers (T4T) as an Aid for Developing Sustained Church Planting Movements (CPMs)*, a dissertation presented to the University of South Africa, 2014.

her new organizational structure to facilitate Church Planting Movements. Her Regent University dissertation, *The Inverted Donut, the Lattice, and the Starfish: Designing the Organizational Architecture for All Nations* aimed at creating "a global organizational architecture for multiplying hubs and church movements."[12]

In 2021, at Southeastern Baptist Theological Seminary, Kevin Greeson explored how Jesus's parable of the sower could provide a road map to movements. Drawing from the work of numerous international Bible scholars, Greeson applied their insights to field-based realities. In doing so, he demonstrated that Jesus's directives in Luke 10 were, in fact, a strategic blueprint for launching a movement.[13]

Some academics were beginning to see that Church Planting Movements were here to stay. Michael T. Cooper was one of them. With a PhD from Trinity Evangelical Divinity School, Cooper had already published four titles when he turned his attention to the missiology of movements.

In 2020 Cooper designed a curriculum for the study of Church Planting Movements that he called *Ephesiology*. Cooper based the name on the apostle Paul's Ephesian ministry referenced in Acts 19:26: "And you see and hear how this fellow Paul has convinced and led astray large numbers here in Ephesus and in practically the whole province of Asia." Later that year, Cooper uploaded his curriculum to the Internet and began offering accredited courses that could earn students a masters in missiology of movements.[14]

---

12. Peifeng Mary Tzen Ho, *The Inverted Donut, the Lattice, and the Starfish: Designing the Organizational Architecture for All Nations*, a doctoral dissertation submitted to Regent University, 2016.

13. Kevin Greeson, *Developing a Strategy Using Jesus's Parable of the Sower for Entering New Ministry Areas*, a dissertation submitted to Southeastern Baptist Theological Seminary, 2021.

14. See Michael T. Cooper's "Ephesiology," at https://www.masterclasses.ephesiology.com, accessed July 1, 2025.

What Kind of Missionary?

As early as the 1990s the IMB's Personnel Selection Department was already asking, "What kind of person makes a good Strategy Coordinator?" Since the question preceded the appearance of the first Church Planting Movements, the movements phenomenon was not initially considered in the evolving profiles of "ideal" Strategy Coordinator candidates.

However, with the rise of movements in the late 1990s, profilers of missionary candidates looked increasingly to the movements themselves for clues to how movement catalysts approached their work. In 2015 Australian Steve Addison published *Pioneering Movements: Leadership that Multiplies Disciples and Churches*.[15] In 2022 missionary researcher Emanuel Prinz penned his own contribution to the subject with *Movement Catalysts: Profiles of an Apostolic Leader*.[16] Based on dialogue with missionaries in pioneer settings who had seen movements, Prinz argued that "wherever you see a movement, you will find a catalyst with a specific set of qualities."[17]

In fact, predicting optimal candidates for CPM catalysts continued to be an elusive target. Effective practitioners came from a variety of backgrounds, secular and ecclesial, military and pacifist, urban and rural, male and female, married and single. These divergent backgrounds lent weight to the observation that CPM catalysts are shaped over time through training and experience rather than possessing inherent qualities that lead to effectiveness.

---

15. Steve Addison, *Pioneering Movements: Leadership that Multiplies Disciples and Churches* (Downers Grove, IL: InterVarsity Press, 2015).

16. Emanuel Prinz, *Movement Catalysts: Profile of an Apostolic Leader* (pub. by author, 2022). Available on Amazon or from the author's website, Globe Mission, https://www.globemission.org/en/missionaries/mission-in-europe/emanuel-prinz/.

17. Prinz, back cover.

Evolving Methods

At the same time, from the earliest gatherings of Strategy Coordinators in the 1990s, one could observe some shared characteristics. Though grounded in Scripture, these pioneers were unbound by convention. There was awareness among these men and women that God was doing something new among the world's least-reached peoples. God used these missionaries' desire to be a part of his multiplying activity to catalyze the first Church Planting Movements. The continued posture of humility and openness to learn new ways—that are actually ancient ways—propels the work forward today.

CPM catalysts are driven by an end vision of their entire people group or urban complex coming to Christ. In philosophical terminology, it is a difference between ontology and teleology. *Ontology* is about who we are; *teleology* is about where we're going. CPM catalysts are teleological in their orientation—focused on the end goal.

In other words, there's a difference between "being a missionary" and "being on mission." In the former case the missionary is the object, a sort of end in themselves. Their definition of what it means to be a missionary merges with their ministry activity, regardless of whether or not it accomplishes the goal of bringing a people group to Christ. In the latter, however, the missionary is an indirect object, a means to an end, and that end is seeing a people group gathered into Christ's kingdom. When missionaries focus on activities that do not contribute to this end vision, they may accomplish many good things, but they fall short of the Great Commission mandate.

This end-vision orientation was reflected in the fundamental question these missionaries asked. Rather than asking, "What can I do?" they fixed their vision on, "What's it going to take?" They subordinated their own ministry to the greater goal of seeing a movement that would bring their entire people group into Christ's kingdom. This paradigm-shifting question compelled these movement catalysts to reach beyond their own limitations to mobilize a comprehensive set of ministries necessary to produce multiplying streams of disciples and churches.

We can see this paradigm shift in the Strategy Coordinator training itself. The earliest Strategy Coordinators were taught to craft a comprehensive strategy built upon five foundational pillars aimed at catalyzing a movement: (1) prayer, (2) evangelism, (3) Scripture, (4) discipleship, and (5) reproducing church formation. Addressing each of these pillars required the missionary to collaborate with scores of partners from across the spectrum of Christian ministries.

By 2000 Strategy Coordinator training sessions were emerging around the world, and they became cross-pollinating laboratories for pioneering missionaries. Out of these interactions a range of movement methodologies took shape: Training for Trainers (T4T),[18] the Camel Method,[19] Discovery Bible Studies,[20] Any-3,[21] and Media to Movements.[22] These methods found their early drafts in Strategy Coordinator training and real-world application before spreading across unreached frontiers.

However, wherever Church Planting Movements took place, it was clear that neither the methods employed nor the

---

18. Ying and Grace Kai, *Ying and Grace Kai's Training for Trainers* (Monument, CO: WIGTake Resources, 2017).

19. Kevin Greeson, *The Camel: How Muslims Are Coming to Faith in Christ!* (Arkadelphia, AR: WIGTake Resources, 2006).

20. David Watson and Paul Watson, *Contagious Disciple Making* (Nashville: Thomas Nelson, 2014).

21. Mike Shipman, *Any-3: Anyone, Anywhere, Anytime* (Monument, CO: WIGTake Resources, 2013).

22. See Jon Ralls, and Chris, Casey, "Media to Movements—A 24:14 Panel Discussion," in *Mission Frontiers*, September-October 2022.

missionaries employing them were an end in themselves. Both the methods and missionaries were vehicles for transmitting the inherent power found within the gospel message.

Concluding Comments

After twenty-five years, Church Planting Movements and their assessments are still in the early stages of their development. Much remains to be learned. As we better discern the ways God is at work in them, our understanding of Church Planting Movements may, in fact, still be in its infancy.

Movement-oriented missions have unleashed gospel power through everyday disciples and simple house churches. Prayerful reliance upon God to shape biblical strategies is turning vast numbers of unreached peoples into disciples and disciple makers. Given the pace at which Church Planting Movements have already transformed the pursuit of the Great Commission, it is not unrealistic to predict that the best practices and understanding of our roles in these movements still await us.

As the proliferation of movements is likely to continue, so too will the need for movement assessments. However, a professional research entity such as the Global Research Department will not always be available to lead these efforts. For this reason, the future of assessments falls to the rest of us—everyday Christians, churches, and sending agencies. Is it really possible to conduct your own movement assessment? That is the topic we will address next.

ELEVEN

DOING YOUR OWN ASSESSMENT

The ultimate purpose of a Church Planting Movement assessment is to advance the kingdom of God. Assessments advance God's kingdom by diving deeply into a reported movement and mining what insights it has to yield. Only then can we confidently determine our own roles going forward.

Who Benefits from an Assessment?

When done well, the benefits extend to the church as a whole, including the agency supporting the ministry, the missionary catalyzing the movement, and the national partners who are the point of the spear in the Kingdom's advance. Most importantly, though, the assessment benefits lost persons within the people group or city who need the gospel and will, as a result of the assessment, gain greater access to the gospel's life-giving power.

Now the hard question: Could you conduct your own CPM assessment? If so, what would it require? Let's walk through the steps needed for you to conduct a DIY, *Do It Yourself*, assessment.

Biblical Basis for Assessment

We must begin with a biblical foundation to ensure that whatever we do aligns with Scripture. As we consider this topic, our thoughts may turn to an Old Testament episode of faithlessness that is associated with a census.

Both 2 Samuel 24 and 1 Chronicles 21 relate the story of King David's census of Israel and Judah's fighting force. David's census angered God because it revealed David's reliance on human strength rather than dependence upon God's provision and protection. In God's disfavor, he leveled a plague against Israel. Does this mean God doesn't like counting? Are assessments contrary to Scripture. Well, no.

Church Planting Movement assessments are quite different. Rather than measure our strength and independence from God, CPM assessments examine where God is working, how he is working, and what our roles should be as we co-labor with him. CPM assessors are more like Joshua and Caleb, the Israelite scouts described in Numbers 13 and 14. These pioneers entered hostile territory, confident of God's providence, and gathered information to join him in his Kingdom advance.

The Gospels also attest to the importance of assessing Kingdom progress. Consider Jesus's parable of the lost sheep in Luke 15:3–7. How could the Good Shepherd know that one of his hundred sheep was lost unless he was keeping count of them? In the same way, CPM catalysts and assessors pursue

Doing Your Own Assessment

lost sheep. In this pursuit they walk in the footsteps of "the Son of Man [who] came to seek and to save the lost" (Luke 19:10).

Likewise, when Jesus sent out seventy-two missionaries in Luke 10, he was not satisfied with simply deploying them; they were sent out to accomplish a mission. Thus, he had them return and report on what they had experienced and accomplished. In this way Jesus was assessing their work.

Following the same pattern, the apostle Paul returned regularly to his flock and corresponded with them to ensure his labors had not been expended in vain. Paul declared, "I do not run like someone running aimlessly; I do not fight like a boxer beating the air" (1 Corinthians 9:26). Paul was on mission. He expected healthy fruit from his labors and measured that fruit both qualitatively and quantitatively throughout his ministry.

Paul further reflected the expectation of reproduction in a letter to his protégé, Timothy. In 2 Timothy 2:2 he wrote, "And the things you have heard me say in the presence of many witnesses entrust to reliable people who will also be qualified to teach others." Paul not only recognized that faithful generations of gospel transmission had delivered the good news to Timothy but that Timothy was to pass it on to others who would continue to do the same.

When Paul learned of deviant doctrine or practice, he not only prayed for his disciples, he also reproved and redirected them in a healthy direction. How could he know if they were deviant without assessing them? As Paul passed on responsibility to future generations, he didn't call his successors "apostles," he called them *episcopoi,* "overseers." In short, they were to be continually overseeing, or assessing, the growth and health of the church movement.

Assessment is a biblical part of being on mission with God.

It is about being accountable to the Lord of the mission, to accomplish his mission.

A Movement Is Reported

Most missionaries and their national partners report regularly on the progress of their work. When a report indicates fourth-generation reproduction, or indicates an exponential increase in churches and disciples, it may be time for an assessment.

The nature of a movement is that it gains its own momentum and grows beyond the missionary's direct involvement. If the work doesn't extend beyond the missionary's control, it is probably not yet a movement. When a missionary sees the work has multiplied beyond his personal oversight, an assessment can help him or her to understand how it is unfolding and what is needed for its continual growth and maturation.

Count the Cost

After you've identified a movement candidate, it's time to weigh the cost of an assessment. Assessments are as expensive as they are valuable. Their cost in time, talent, and treasure is considerable. Jesus admonished: "Suppose one of you wants to build a tower. Won't you first sit down and estimate the cost to see if you have enough money to complete it? For if you lay the foundation and are not able to finish it, everyone who sees it will ridicule you, saying, 'This person began to build and wasn't able to finish'" (Luke 14:28–30).

The paragraphs that follow will help you measure the cost of an effective CPM assessment. As you walk through these elements, prayerfully consider both the cost and the importance.

Doing Your Own Assessment

Identify a Team Leader
While an assessment will include multiple individuals and as many informants as possible, the buck has to stop with someone, and this someone is the team leader. The team leader must be willing to invest time and effort as he or she manages details and coordinates the many contributors to the process.

Clarify Your Target
Before you get too far into the assessment process, make sure to clarify the task before you. What are you looking for? Two definitions are critically important: (1) the definition of a movement, and (2) the definition of the population you will assess.

Though you should remain open to surprises, it helps to begin with a working definition of a Church Planting Movement or Disciple Making Movement. The one we've used thus far provides a good starting point: "A CPM is the rapid and multiplicative increase of indigenous churches planting churches within a given people group or population segment." Similarly, a DMM (Disciple Making Movement) is the rapid and multiplicative increase of disciples reproducing disciples that spreads through a people group or population segment."[1] This is what you're looking for.

Next, you'll want to clarify your research target. If you're tackling a geographic region—such as a state, city, or province—you'll need to account for its ethnic and linguistic diversity. Make sure you're not confusing what's happening in Christian enclaves with what's happening among the unreached in that region. Appendix A at the end of this book will help you with both tasks.

The sharpest filter, even within urban centers, continues to be an ethnolinguistic one. You can discover the ethnolinguistic

---
1. See chapter one: "What Are We Talking About?"

composition of a group by asking two questions: (1) what is their heart language, and (2) what is their ethnicity? Ethnicity includes the religious, cultural, and historic traits that your people group shares.

Once you've clarified both your CPM definition and the scope of the population segment you're assessing, you're ready for the next step.

Secure Field Collaboration

A good assessment requires good field partners. These partners may be members of local churches, new believers from the movement itself, or missionaries reporting a movement within the population segment. The most thorough assessments include a 360-degree survey combining input from all three. It's important to remember that those on the field are your primary clients. You are serving them with an assessment, not auditing them as a supervisor.

When an assessment begins from the West or an outside entity, a collaborative spirit becomes all the more important. You can foster this spirit, by helping your in-country partners understand that you share with them the vision of bringing the lost to faith in Jesus Christ, rather than a desire to audit their work.

Your field partners will be essential in many ways. Good partners can assist with demographic profiles; providing translators, transporters, visas, food and lodging, lists of churches and interview sites; and interpreting data in light of local worldviews. They can guide you through security challenges posed by hostile forces. They can segmentize the movement into measurable components such as neighborhoods or districts. Or they may suggest surveying streams of new churches that trace their origins back to specific trainers, churches, or methodologies employed.

A random sampling of informants is critical to obtaining the most accurate assessment. The simplest way to achieve a random sampling is to list as many churches as possible, then select at random the ones to be assessed, such as every third or fifth church in the list.

If a random sampling is not possible, try to conduct a 360-degree assessment that includes: (1) churches from within the movement; (2) a mix of male and female informants, urban and rural, leaders and laity, young and old, newer and more mature believers, and, when appropriate, literate and nonliterate; (3) informants from other evangelicals working in the city or among the people group; and (4) leaders from traditional churches that may not be directly involved in the lay-led movements occurring around them.

You will likely never get as many informants as you want; but the more you get, particularly from random samples, the more accurate your picture will be of the purported movement.

Develop Your Assessment Questionnaire

Keep in mind the questionnaire paradox: the longer your questionnaire, the more data you can acquire, but the fewer informants you will be able to interview. So, choose your questions wisely. Your questions should consist of a mix of what you want to know and what your field partners want to know. Start with your core questions built around the two axes of quality and quantity.

How do qualitative questions look? These might include: (1) Can you share with me your testimony? (2) Can you tell me about your church? (3) How did you come to faith? (4) Where, when, and how does your church worship? (5) How do you and your church use the Bible?

Quantitative questions address the size and growth rates of the movement. These might include: (1) To the best of your knowledge, how many believers are among your people or in your city? (2) How many have you led to Christ? (3) How many churches have you (or your church) started in the past year, three years, and so on? (4) What is the size of your church? (5) What is the typical size of a church among your people group or in your city?

Again, the appendices at the end of this book will help. They will likely provide you with more questions than you need, but they offer a good starting point as you develop your own assessment questionnaire.

Research Before Assessing

Before you venture to the field, develop a profile of the people group or city you aim to survey. The more you know before you travel, the more you can learn after you arrive. If you're fortunate your field partners can provide an ethnographic or urban profile of the locale in which the movement or movements are taking place. Nonetheless, you will want to gather additional information that is readily available today through Internet-based research. A few Google and Wikipedia searches will give you some basic demographic data as well as provide a bibliography of published sources for further investigation.

Assemble a Team

The composition of your assessment team is critical to the success of your survey. The best assessment teams include: local partners who are knowledgeable about the scope of the movement; professional missionaries from other fields; the individuals who reported the movement and sought outside counsel; and savvy, yet curious, inquirers who do not have a vested interest in the outcome. By vested interest we aren't saying they are disinterested—otherwise, why would they agree to this time-laden process—but rather, they are not biased to prove or disprove the existence or nature of the movement. Finally, if you want to interview both men and women, you'll need both men and women on your assessment team.

As you share with your team the research profile you have developed, ask them to pray for the people being assessed, for the missionaries on the field, and for one another. Prayer is the means by which assessors come to see their work from God's perspective. Prayer is also essential to protecting this important assessment task from the many obstacles that Satan will levy against them.

The Days Before

Before the team assembles on the field, make sure they are all informed regarding the working definition of a movement, the advance research profile of the target field, the questionnaire that will be used, and the security parameters of the movement context.

Before the assessment begins, once your team is gathered in a launch location, prepare your teammates for the work ahead and pray through its various components. Remind your team that this is not an audit by a superior of a subordinate. The goal is to discern both quality and quantity through humble engagement of brothers and sisters who have indicated that God is doing an extraordinary work in their community.

Be Humble when Asking Questions

Coach your teammates to approach their interviews with a healthy measure of humility. This is not an interrogation! Praying with your informants reminds them that you are one of them. Ask open-ended questions that don't presuppose the answers you are seeking, and don't be surprised if you receive answers you didn't anticipate. Your goal is to get a clear picture, not a predetermined one.

You may want to organize your assessment team into pairs, each with an accompanying translator and driver. If your context does not allow you to take notes during interviews, take the time as soon as possible to record what you've heard. After each interview, confirm what you've heard with your translator and assessment partner to assure accuracy.

Debrief Your Team

At the end of each survey day, you will be exhausted. Nevertheless, it is important to conclude each day with a team debriefing of your impressions. The daily debrief will not be comprehensive or conclusive but will provide an opportunity for you and your teammates to learn from one another. The debriefing should include five questions: (1) What were your impressions of your informants? (2) What obstacles did you encounter? (3) How did you overcome them? (4) How might the questionnaire be adjusted to get a better picture? (5) How can you be more effective tomorrow?

After your field surveys are complete, it's time for the team to digest their findings. This begins with a dialogue as each two-member team shares their findings with the group. What were your general impressions? Was there a movement? What led you to that conclusion? Were there signs of deception? If so, in what ways? What conflicting elements did you find in your assessment? What strengths and weaknesses of the ministry did you identify?

At the end of the field assessment, each team member will submit their findings in writing to the team leader. The team leader will read through the submissions to verify his or her understanding of what the team members observed.

Doing Your Own Assessment

As the field portion of the assessment process concludes, spend some time together in prayer. Pray together for wisdom and insight. Pray for God's work within the population you are assessing; and pray for your team leader, who now has the task of compiling and analyzing the input.

Compile Your Findings

The team leader now has the delightful, yet demanding, task of sifting through the data. The team leader may wish to enter the data into spreadsheets that can be cross-referenced for comparison. From this compiled data, the team leader will be able to determine whether or not a movement or movements are underway.

If a movement is discovered, the team leader should use the collected data to make educated estimates of its size and scope. Does it correlate to the reports that initiated the assessment in the first place? The team leader will also be able to discern important patterns regarding strengths and weaknesses in the movement or where and how it fell short of being a movement.

Generate Two Reports

In most instances, the team leader will generate two reports. One report will be as exhaustive as possible. This comprehensive report will also be confidential. It will include contextual information about the people group(s) or urban center(s) that were assessed. It will describe the methodology of the assessment and the individuals who comprised the assessment team. The comprehensive report will offer valuable insights into both the quantity and quality of the work. In this report the team leader will generate recommendations to address both accelerants to the movement and challenges that jeopardize the growth and health of the movement.

The confidential report is not for publication. The primary client for the confidential report is the emerging church that was assessed. However, it likely contains information that might undermine the work if it were to be circulated. For this reason the confidential report should be shared only with those who are directly involved in the work itself.

The missionary or national partner on the field is the best person to determine who should receive the confidential report. From this wealth of information the field leader can filter out security-sensitive information and use it to encourage, correct, strengthen, or redirect the work without sabotaging the advance of the Kingdom in what may be a hostile environment.

The second report is an executive overview, a redacted summary of the movement that eliminates any information that might damage the movement should it fall into the wrong hands. This typically means deleting the names of individuals and places that need to remain discreet.

With these safeguards in place the team leader can still create a valuable executive summary that profiles the setting where the assessment took place. The executive summary should be sufficient to establish the existence or nonexistence of a movement and the reason for reaching this conclusion. It should also include strategic recommendations that can inform resource allocations moving forward.

Serve Your Clients

Before sharing the findings the team leader should discuss them with the field point person who leads the work. This field point person can help the team leader avoid misunderstanding.

Remember, both parties are capable of confirmation bias that could lead to faulty conclusions.

Once the team leader and field partner are in agreement, the assessment reports can serve as a mirror to the movement and reveal trends, patterns, strengths, and weaknesses. The field point person is then empowered to use this mirror to reflect on how best to move forward toward the vision of seeing their people come to the fullness of new life in Christ.

The assessment team leader will also want to communicate the executive summary to stakeholders in the movement. These stakeholders include ministry partners who are contributing to the work. Strategic stakeholders may include Bible translators, broadcast ministries, churches, and foundations. Sharing the findings with these partners allows alignment to form around the key questions: "What is happening?" and "How can we best participate in the ways that God is working?"

Conclusion

If after reaching this point you are still interested in pursuing your own assessment, you just might be the kind of person who *should* conduct an assessment. Church Planting Movement assessments are not easy; but, as we've seen, they can be well worth it.

Someone noted, "If the body of Christ only knew what the body of Christ knows, we just might know enough to do the work of Christ in the world." Imagine how much the global body of Christ has learned, is learning, and has yet to learn! While we will not know the whole of how God is at work in frontier movements until Christ does his "Great Assessment" at the end of time, we have much to learn today. As you pursue your own CPM assessments, you add your own contribution to the growing knowledge of the body of Christ.

While much remains to be learned, the past quarter century of CPM assessments has already taught us a lot. In the next chapter we will review the findings of twenty-eight movement surveys and draw from them some answers to the questions we introduced at the beginning of this book.

TWELVE

EVIDENCE THAT DEMANDS A VERDICT

We began this journey with the question, Are Church Planting Movements real? Hidden within that question are the underlying questions: Are Church Planting Movements a fabrication? and How can we know? Rather than reveal our own confirmation bias, let's revisit our definition of Church Planting Movements and then let the evidence speak for itself.

We defined Church Planting Movements as rapidly multiplying indigenous churches planting churches that sweep through people groups or population segments. Now for the evidence. What did our survey of twenty-eight Church Planting Movement assessments reveal?

The evidence, gathered over nearly a quarter century of on-site investigations, can be clustered under three categories: (1) Confirmed Church Planting Movements, (2) Confirmed Non-Church Planting Movements, and (3) Something In Between. Let's take a closer look at each category.

Confirmed Church Planting Movements

The International Mission Board's investigation of twenty-eight reported movements revealed eleven indisputable instances of rapidly multiplying indigenous churches planting churches sweeping through a people group or population. These movements resulted in hundreds of thousands of new Christians among some of the world's least-evangelized peoples.

Clearly assessed Church Planting Movements were confirmed among:

1. The Bhojpuri of India
2. Bengali Muslims of Bangladesh
3. Buddhists of Cambodia
4. Cubans
5. A Berber people group in North Africa
6. The Adivasi of South Asia
7. The Kekchi of Guatemala
8. An urban megalopolis in Asia
9. The Foro Muslims in an African nation
10. The Shistani people from the Middle East
11. The South Asian people of Quellestan

Before we depart from this list of confirmed Church Planting Movements, let's recall a few conclusions about each one.

The assessment of the Bhojpuri revealed, despite the field missionary's extraordinary report, he was actually underestimating the number of new churches and disciples that had emerged in his ministry. The 50,000 disciples and 2,600 churches that he had reported were actually determined by on-site assessment to be somewhere between 224,000 and 374,000 disciples meeting in an estimated 3,277 to 5,461 churches.

The turning of Muslims to Christ in Bangladesh instigated

an on-site assessment and yielded similar conclusions. The missionary had been conservative and underestimated the number of Muslim-background believers by 80 percent.

The movement that emerged among Cambodian Buddhists had Baptist roots before bursting out of its denominational confines. The number of believers in the country exploded from fewer than 23,000 in 1990 to more than half a million in 2024.

Despite restrictions on missionary access, and internal obstacles posed by the atheistic Communist government in Cuba, a Baptist movement of new disciples and churches swelled from 654 churches in 1995 to 5,657 churches in 2002. We don't have to speculate about these numbers. They were confirmed by 400 on-site interviews, and eventually by the Ministry of Religious Affairs itself.

Rumors of a movement among a particular Berber people group in a hostile North African country were replaced by the confirmation of thousands of new Berber Christians. The onsite survey team found scores of new churches and thousands of baptized believers in major urban centers and scattered throughout the country's interior.

Through the same process, interviews with 334 randomly selected informants from the tribal Adivasi people of South Asia uncovered a rapidly growing indigenous movement of new disciples and churches. Their numbers increased from no more than 10,000 baptized believers in 1995 to more than 127,000 in 2002.

In a less restrictive yet largely neglected people in Guatemala's interior, missionaries reported movement growth from 9,457 Kekchi Christians in 1993 to 34,000 in 2004. Their report was verified by a team of on-site assessors who spent weeks interviewing 260 randomly selected informants.

One of the more remarkable movements was in an urban

megalopolis in Asia, where the Kais reported their T4T network had started approximately 44,000 churches comprised of 483,000 baptized disciples. After 400 to 500 randomly selected interviews in multiple languages across two provinces, the assessment team determined that the Kais had underreported the size of the movement by 40 percent!

Among the Foro people, whose identity was virtually synonymous with Islam, a single missionary woman reported a movement that had produced 3,000 Foro conversions to Christianity. On-site assessment revealed that she had, in fact, underreported the reality by 65 percent.

Speculation about the implausible growth of Christianity among the Middle Eastern Shistani people led to a four-phased assessment that traced multiple streams of new disciples and churches across seven countries. Interviews and on-site investigations led to the verification of multiple streams of Shistani believers scattered around the world.

Finally, there was the skeptically received annual report of 14,190 new church starts among a predominantly Hindu people in Quellestan that prompted a trustee-supervised assessment. After three weeks interviewing 384 selected churches—by 14 missionaries and 4 trustees—the trustees determined that only one of the churches no longer met. Qualitative investigations of church members revealed that 75 percent of the new believers could quote Scripture, 79 percent had discipled someone else, and 70 percent reported daily engagement with Scripture.

All together these eleven movements had seen well over two million baptized believers gathered into multiplying new churches. These eleven assessments left no doubt as to the reality of Church Planting Movements, rapidly multiplying indigenous churches planting churches that sweep through people groups or population segments. As a trustee assessment team member confessed: *they are real.*

Evidence that Demands a Verdict

Confirmed Non-Church Planting Movements

However, of equal importance, were eleven other assessments that confirmed the absence of a Church Planting Movement. One of these non-movements took place among the Olduwar people of South Asia. Though the Olduwar ministry exhibited many characteristics of a movement, rather than producing rapidly multiplying indigenous house churches, the thousands of new Olduwar believers had migrated into thirty-nine traditional churches of the Koinonia Network. Had an assessment not been conducted, this unexpected detour would likely have gone undetected.

Assessments also revealed the absence of movements among nine sub-Saharan people groups. Three of these peoples—the Yani, the Koro, and the Kusho—exhibited significant growth in a challenging situation; nevertheless, the assessment team's survey determined that none of them had yet tipped over into a movement. Five other Subsa people groups—the Walu, Sobay, Anko, Daimu, and Brosh—had actually shown a decline in numbers between what was reported in 2012 and what the assessment found in 2016. One of the people groups, the Fan, left the assessment team unsure of what its actual numbers were. In each of the surveys, though, the assessors found aspects to celebrate as well as course corrections that could strengthen the ministries.

It is worth noting that even though the nine sub-Saharan ministries reported by MovementCatalysts were not movements, they were also not insignificant. In combination, these works brought more than 26,000 new disciples into 636 new churches in the midst of some of the world's least-reached and most hostile contexts. Even the absence of a movement is not the same as a failure. When you shoot for the stars and only hit the moon, you've still hit the moon—not bad.

Like the Fan assessment, the team that revisited the Bengali

Muslim movement was left with ambiguous results. Though most of the members of the 2004 Bengali assessment agreed that something significant was happening, quite possibly a Church Planting Movement, their research also detected misinformation from their informants, leading them to suspend any conclusions about the scope and nature of what was underway. Only because their assessment methods were sound, were they able to avoid reaching misleading conclusions.

Something In Between

Just as important as the confirmation of movements or non-movements were the six assessments that revealed something in between. Four of the urban assessments in chapter seven—Wu City, Lo City, So City, and Co City—disclosed the presence of what the assessors deemed "emerging movements." Each of these urban ministries had experienced rapid multiplication of new disciples and churches and was tracking toward a movement. Equally evident were significant challenges that might yet derail these works. In each instance the assessment teams highlighted strengths and weaknesses and made recommendations that would help the ministries make progress moving forward.

As we noted in the non-movements summary, the goal of rapidly multiplying indigenous churches planting churches that sweep through people groups or population segments led to some laudable results. In less than five years these four urban ministries produced approximately 304 new churches in multiple streams comprising more than 4,000 new disciples. They also taught the Strategy Coordinators pursuing movements how to overcome obstacles and better navigate the unique challenges of reaching a rapidly urbanizing world.

Similarly, two South Asian ministries—the Basara and

Bhow peoples—showed remarkable growth among previously neglected people groups. Nevertheless, the assessments also revealed significant impediments to their qualitative and quantitative future. The surveys held up a mirror to the work and provided critical insights that might otherwise have been missed. Based upon the assessment findings the Strategy Coordinators were able to make strategic adjustments, which enabled them to avoid pitfalls that threatened the health of their ministry and the churches they produced.

The Truth Is Out There

The evidence of CPM assessments has answered our question, Are Church Planting Movements real? The evidence is undeniable. Assessors asked extensive questions to discover both the size and nature of the movements. Their efforts at gathering random samplings across broad segments of the movements left no doubt these peoples and cities were exhibiting rapidly multiplying indigenous churches planting churches that were sweeping through their population.

The answer to our second question, Are Church Planting Movements fabrications? is more nuanced. As we saw in the second Bengali Muslim assessment, deception can be a part of the mix. But, as we have also seen, assessments are excellent tools in revealing false information. Without assessments we would be left in the dark. By now, it is easy to answer our last question: "How do you know?"

As you might have guessed, the answer to the last question is Church Planting Movement assessments. Assessments can cut through the haze as they explore both the size and quality of reported movements. In some instances—such as the Bhojpuri, Adivasi, Foro, and Megalopolis assessments—the assessments revealed numbers even larger than what the missionary reported. Other surveys, such as the Quellestan assessment, revealed a measure of fidelity to Scripture that exceeded that of many U.S. churches. In every case, thoughtful assessments revealed new information and provided missionaries and their partners with ways they could better guide their unfolding ministry.

In addition to answering the three questions posed at the beginning of this chapter, three additional lessons emerge from our review of the evidence.

First, we should not be afraid to ask questions. Sincere questions are necessary for evaluating the nature and scope of movements. As such, questions are an invaluable resource in the church's toolkit.

Second, we must acknowledge that what we uncover in the study of Church Planting Movements is rarely binary in nature. There is much more to learn than simply: (1) yes, it is a CPM, or (2) no, it is not a CPM. Church Planting Movements offer a wealth of new insights and provide us with a texture of understanding that is much more complex than simply yes or no. As we plumb the depths of these movements, we become better equipped to strengthen our strategies and correct our shortcomings.

Finally, Church Planting Movements and their assessments only make sense in light of their shared goal, which is the fulfillment of Christ's commission to make disciples of all nations. Weighed against this goal, both movements and assessments are imperfect. In combination, though, as means to a shared end, they hold great promise in expediting the fulfillment of the Great Commission.

Diving deeply into qualitative and quantitative questions about movements provides us with new insights into how God is at work in them and how we can best participate. Assessing the realities within Church Planting Movements equips us to co-labor with God in those movements, avoiding pitfalls and contributing to the movement's growth in both depth and breadth.

But there remains one very important question we must not miss, and we'll address it in the final chapter.

THIRTEEN

WHERE DO WE GO FROM HERE?

Our remaining question is this: Where do we go from here? The answer is up to you. Moving forward requires a step of faith, an essential part of any Christian's commitment to reaching unreached people groups at the ends of the earth. But today, faith-filled pioneers need not enter the darkness without hope or purpose. They are, or can be, participants in multiplying movements of people coming to Christ.

Whether you personally see a movement or not, you can be assured that God is on the side of all nations becoming Christ's disciples. As the apostle Peter wrote, "The Lord is not slow in keeping his promise, as some understand slowness. Instead he is patient with you, *not wanting anyone to perish*, but everyone to come to repentance" (2 Peter 3:9, italics added).

Did you catch that? God does not desire that *anyone* would perish, but that *everyone* would come to repentance. This promise, this assurance, is what propels pioneering missionaries to leave home, learn new languages, and share the gospel with people groups who rarely value their presence. Some missionaries toil for a lifetime without seeing much in the way of response. Others, though, have seen movements, and we have much to learn from both exemplars of faithfulness.

As you've learned from the many examples in this book, Church Planting Movements are an undeniable reality in the world today, and they are a worthwhile aspiration. They hold great hope for penetrating the very ends of the earth with the gospel of Jesus Christ and transforming the kingdoms of this world into the kingdom of God.

This explains why the reality of Church Planting Movements is so unsettling for many Christians. If Church Planting Movements are real, how can we afford to ignore or oppose them? How can we dismiss something God is doing that is bringing millions of new believers into discipleship-based churches among the world's least-reached peoples?

The haunting question for us is: Will *we* be a part of what God is doing in these movements? If not, perhaps God will raise up others who will be his willing co-laborers. But if we do not respond to the challenge, it is our loss. God is not dependent on us, but he has chosen to accomplish his purposes through those who are obedient. God continues to extend his work through those who say to him, "Here am I, Lord. Send me."

Our Challenge

Gone are the days when an honest critic could simply dismiss reports of movements as fabrications or illusions. Gone, too, are the days when every report was accepted at face value. God has used Church Planting Movements and their assessments to provide the church with a tool, a torch to light our way, as we seek

Where Do We Go from Here?

to fulfill his Great Commission. Yet skeptics will persist, as they always have.

In Luke 16:19–31 Jesus related the fate of a rich man, languishing in torment, who begged Abraham to send Lazarus to warn his family, for he had five brothers. Yet Abraham ". . . said to him, 'If they do not listen to Moses and the Prophets, they will not be convinced even if someone rises from the dead'" (vv. 28, 31). In the same way, assessments of Church Planting Movements will not convince everyone.

Perhaps the greatest skeptic in Jesus's day wasn't from outside the faith community but from within it. This was the apostle Thomas who said, in short, "I will not believe unless I see it for myself." However, once he had seen Jesus for himself he was convinced, and he was transformed.

Church tradition tells us that after his experience with the resurrected Lord, Thomas became a missionary and took the gospel as far as India. The movement fruit that Thomas catalyzed two thousand years ago continues to flourish to this day, with countless indigenous churches planting churches throughout South Asia. Today, millions of Indian Christians trace their lineage back to Thomas's life-changing response to the risen Lord.

Perhaps, like Thomas, you were once a skeptic; but now you have seen. The question is this: What will you do with this knowledge?

To pursue a Church Planting Movement is no fool's errand. It is nothing less than aligning ourselves with God's desire that none should perish. This is God's heart for the nations. What about us? What is our heart?

Over the past quarter century, countless men and women have participated in Church Planting Movements and their assessments. They have seen, analyzed, and reported on what they have found. This is their gift to the church, providing us with valuable tools to advance Christ's kingdom and navigate the farthest reaches of the Great Commission.

Their legacy leaves us with the question, Now that we have seen, how will we respond?

APPENDICES

TOOLS YOU CAN USE

APPENDIX A

REFINING URBAN ASSESSMENTS

The Challenge of Urban Assessments

Cities are easy, right? After all, everyone is gathered in one place and not scattered across hundreds of villages and hamlets in hard-to-access locations. Well, while urban assessment teams have some advantages, such as reliable transportation and predictable infrastructure (think running water and toilets), cities also pose their own challenges to accurate assessments.

Unlike assessments conducted among a single unreached people group, urban contexts typically pose a more complex ethnolinguistic landscape. While some cities are comprised largely of a single dominant language group, this façade can also hide the existence of multiple other people groups within its boundaries. This is why creating an ethnolinguistic profile of a city is an important step in the pre-assessment research. An assessment that fails to examine the various ethnic enclaves of a city can easily present a skewed or misleading picture of the true state of the unfinished task.

Most of China, for example, presents a relatively homogenous population with 91 percent Han Chinese and 71 percent who speak some dialect of Mandarin Chinese.[1] Other countries, though, such as Indonesia and India, are extremely diverse in both language and ethnicity, thus requiring more ethnolinguistically informed assessments.

By way of example, the city of Bangalore, in the Indian state of Karnataka, is a rapidly growing metropolis of 14 million inhabitants. A survey of Christianity in the city reveals thousands of churches and some 785,000 Christians. With nearly 6 percent of the city claiming Christianity as their religion, a superficial assessment might lead one to conclude that the city is largely "reached" by the gospel. However, this Christian population belies a more complex reality.

A closer look reveals that almost all of Bangalore's Christians come from four ethnolinguistic communities: Tamilians, Nagas, Telugu-speakers from Andhra Pradesh, and Keralite Malayalam-speakers. However, non-Christian populations in the city include more than five million Kannada-speaking Hindus with very little work among them. Even more neglected are nearly two million Urdu-speaking Muslims, who are often the last to be approached with the gospel.[2] Any assessment that fails to account for ethnolinguistic diversity will result in a deficient understanding of what is really happening in the city.

---

1. See "What Languages are Spoken in China?" at https://www.worldatlas.com/articles/what-languages-are-spoken-in-china.html accessed June 17, 2025.

2. Religious and demographic information is derived from two sources. *World Population Review*, "Bangalore", https://worldpopulationreview.com/world-cities/bangalore-population, and "Bangalore" on Wikipedia at: https://en.wikipedia.org/wiki/Bangalore, both sites accessed on July 11, 2024.

360-Degree Assessments

The five urban assessments profiled in chapter seven described CPM assessments in a conflicted context. Due to intense security constraints in the Asian country, the assessors determined that Jim Slack's 121-question assessment guide was impractical.[3] They opted, instead, for a more focused 360-degree assessment that included informants from traditional churches, new house churches, and other evangelicals working in the city. While this approach did not always yield a true random sampling, it did overcome government surveillance while still producing insightful results.

The Asia urban assessment teams employed ten key topics of inquiry that they translated into the local language and committed to memory. Their points of inquiry were specific, yet open-ended, allowing informants to respond in their own words. Here is the actual list they addressed:

1. Tell us how you first heard about Jesus.
2. Tell us how you accepted Jesus.
3. Tell us about your baptism.
4. Tell us about when you meet with other believers.
5. Tell us how leaders are chosen and trained.
6. Tell us about your training.
7. How does your group deal with crises?
8. How does your group do evangelism?
9. How are other churches being started?
10. Tell us about challenges your group faces.

---

3. The security concerns in the Asian country in question were justified. The government surveilled virtually every aspect of the society, which posed real threats to missionary efforts. A decade after these case studies were generated, the government exposed and expelled all IMB missionaries from the country.

Regarding the composition of the assessment teams, the regional leader typically chose four missionaries, two men and two women who were proficient in the language, each of whom had assignments outside the assessed city. At least one of the team members had some experience with a Church Planting Movement.

Evident in the urban assessments was the attention given to discipleship within the context of healthy reproducing churches. In each of the assessed urban movements, the teams were able to confirm that the Kais' Training for Trainers (T4T) methodology was instrumental in launching new disciples and churches.

Conclusions

Urban Church Planting Movement assessments present unique challenges. In high-security contexts they may not afford the team the luxury of true random sampling or of asking 121 questions of every informant. This challenge can be mitigated, though, if the team (1) has done a pre-assessment profiling of the city, (2) knows what they are looking for with more targeted questions aimed at CPM distinctives, and (3) are able to gather informants who reflect a 360-degree investigation of the work—including historic churches, other evangelicals working in the city, and the house-church streams themselves. This type of 360-degree analysis allows the team to take a deep dive into what the field missionary has reported both in terms of quality and quantity.

APPENDIX B

DR. JIM SLACK'S CPM ASSESSMENT

Questionnaire in 2005

Developed by Church Growth Analyst Jim Slack and the Global Research Department of the International Mission Board, SBC

Part 1: Description of the UPG or City (6 data points)

1. Name of Group or other population segment (alternative names)
2. Location(s)
3. Population
4. Language(s)
5. Religion(s)
6. History of Christian Work

Part 2: Description of Informants (9 data points)

1. Gender
2. Age
3. Residence (e.g., province, village, etc.)
4. Highest educational level attained
5. Language(s) spoken
6. How long has the informant been a Christian?
7. Does the informant have a leadership role in the church? If so, what?
8. Other relevant demographic information regarding the informant

Part 3: History, Nature, and Extent of the Movement (4 data points)

1. Describe the history of the movement. Include key individuals, groups, and events.
2. Nature of the Movement: Is this a CPM?

A church planting movement is a sustained, rapid multiplication of churches planting churches within a given population segment. The following items are essential for determining whether or not a church planting movement is underway.

A. Sustainability
A key factor that separates church planting movements from short-lived increases in church plants (such as those resulting from an evangelistic crusade or church planting campaigns) is sustainability. Once begun, church planting movements are not reliant on significant outside initiative, assistance, or resources. The following items are critical for answering the question of sustainability.

Dr. Jim Slack's CPM Assessment

1. Evangelism, discipleship, and church planting DNA (17 data points)

   Church planting movements are dependent upon the evangelism, discipleship, and church planting efforts of church members.

   a) Who in the church is doing the evangelism, discipleship, and church planting? What percentage of church membership is engaged in evangelism? Discipling others? Church planting?
   b) How soon after coming to faith are individuals sharing their faith and discipling others? Planting churches?
   c) Who provides training and mentoring in the process of evangelism, discipleship, and church planting? What is the frequency and duration of such training and mentoring?
   d) What is the content, format (formal vs. informal, individual/small group/conference, etc.), and location of such training and mentoring?

2. Selection and training of church leadership (11 data points)

   a) Who is receiving leadership training within churches?
   b) Are churches choosing their own leadership? How?
   c) Are churches identifying multiple leaders in each church?
   d) What roles do leaders play? What things can only be done by leaders?
   e) How are leaders trained? Who teaches them?

f) What is the content, format, and location of such training?

3. Indigeneity (10 data points)

   a) Are churches finding places to meet without outside funding?
   b) Is leadership coming from within the local church?
   c) Is the local church handling its own celebration of the Lord's Supper and baptism?
   d) Are members in the church self-feeding from God's Word? How do church members study God's Word?
   e) Is the worship and ministry language of the church compatible with that of the community?
   f) What are the sources, transmission, and uses of outside funding?
   g) Are the churches producing their own music?
   h) What languages are used in the worship and ministry of the church?
   i) Are the churches finding ways to take the gospel to others?

B. Rapid Multiplication (3 data points)

By definition, church planting movements involve rapid multiplication. How rapid is "rapid"? In a church planting movement, the majority of churches reproduce within twelve months. Demographic information collected above may reveal that only particular segments of the larger people group are experiencing a CPM.

1. What percentage of churches are reproducing each year?

2. How long does it take for new churches to reproduce?
3. What percentage of new churches are reproducing within twelve months?

C. Extent of the Movement (4 data points)

An important part of the work of the assessment team is to determine the extent of the movement. This may present one of the greatest challenges to the team. The nature of the research methodology employed as well as that of the information available to the team will greatly affect the reliability of this determination. Some possibilities include: a) a census of churches in the movement; b) a sufficiently-large random sample of churches in the movement; c) written records or reports regarding growth of the movement; d) estimates by leaders and/or members. The team should always aim to make the most accurate estimate possible given the constraints of the situation in which it is conducting its assessment.

The Confidential Report provides definitions of many terms used in this assessment. Carefully note distinctions between various categories (e.g. the difference between "churches" and "outreach groups"). (Total of 33 data points)

A. Total churches: 1) This year? 2) One year ago? 3) Five years ago? 4) Ten years ago? 5) Average annual growth rates?
B. Total number of new churches planted: 1) This year? 2) Last year?
C. Total membership: 1) This year? 2) Five years ago? 3) Ten years ago? 4) Average annual growth rates?
D. Total number of baptisms: 1) This year? 2) Last year?
E. Total number of outreach groups: 1) This year? 2) One

year ago? 3) Five years ago? 4) Ten years ago? 5) Average annual growth rates?
F. Total number of new outreach groups started: 1) This year? 2) Last year?
G. Total number of missionaries sent from this group to another people group within the same country: 1) This year? 2) Last year? 3) Five years ago?
H. Total number of missionaries sent from this group to a people group in another country: 1) This year? 2) Last year? 3) Five years ago?
I. Geographic Distribution 1) What is the geographic distribution of the movement? 2) Are there any places or segments of the group where the movement is not spreading? 3) Why?
J. Boundaries 1) Note any ethnic, 2) linguistic, 3) cultural, or 4) other significant boundaries the movement has crossed.

APPENDIX C

CPM ASSESSMENT QUESTIONNAIRE

From the 2022 IMB Assessment of Quellestan

Developed by Director Wilson Geisler and the Global Research Department of the International Mission Board, SBC

A. Interview Questions

1. How old are you (what is your age)?
2. What is your mother language?
3. Please tell us when you first heard about Jesus.
4. Please tell us how you first heard about Jesus.
    a. When did you first hear?
    b. From whom?
    c. How many other believers are in your family?

5. Please tell us why you decided to follow Jesus.
   a. When did you first decide to follow Jesus?
   b. Who is Jesus?
   c. Describe how your life has changed since you became a follower of Jesus.
6. Please tell us the gospel.
   a. What is God's *Ek Rasta* (meaning "One Way"— the evangelism, discipleship, and church planting program developed by the missionaries)?
   b. How should people respond to the gospel? How do they become followers of Jesus?
7. Are you baptized?
   a. When were you baptized? (How long have you been baptized?)
   b. Who baptized you?
   c. What does baptism mean to you?
8. How often do you read or listen to Scripture?
   a. Do you have a Bible or some way to listen to Scripture in your own language?
   b. Would you please share a Scripture with me from memory?
9. What is the church?
   a. Who is your church?
   b. How often does your church meet?
   c. How many people usually meet together?
   d. Where does the church meet?
   e. Are you a leader in the church?
10. Have you ever discipled anyone else?
    a. What did you disciple them about?
    b. Have your disciples discipled anyone else?
    c. Have you started any Bible study groups?
11. Describe your daily walk with Jesus.
    a. When do you pray and read/listen to the Bible?

CPM Assessment Questionnaire

   b. When do you share the gospel of Jesus with other people?
   c. How do you show love to other people?
12. Before you decided to follow Christ, what was your religion and caste?

B. Church Quantitative and Qualitative Assessment (Mixed Method Assessment)

1. Is the church still active and meeting?
2. Name of church?
3. Date the church started?
4. Does this church self-identify (consider themselves) a church?
5. What is this church's generation?
6. Does this church have leaders?
   a. What are the leaders' names?
   b. What are the genders of the leaders?
7. Does this church practice believer's baptism?
   a. Does the leader or person giving the baptism come from inside or outside the church?
8. Does this church practice the Lord's Supper?
   a. Does the leader or person giving the Lord's Supper come from inside or outside the church?
9. How many attend this group or church?
10. How many that attend are believers?
11. How many that attend are baptized?
12. Is Basic Discipleship being taught to all members?
13. Does this church collect tithes and offerings?
14. Does this church regularly worship together?
15. How often does this church meet?—Once a week, more than once a week, less than once a week?

16. Does this church have regular teaching or preaching?
    a. How often is there regular teaching or preaching?
    b. Does the leader giving teaching or preaching come from inside or outside the church?

C. Church Member Qualitative Assessment

1. What is the person's name?
2. What is their gender?
3. What is their age?
4. What is this person's people group, language, and religious background?
5. Is this person a leader in the church?
6. Does this person understand the gospel and why they believed?
7. Is this person baptized?
8. How often does this person read or listen to Scripture?
9. Does this person have Scripture memorized?
10. Does this person have a clear understanding of church?
11. Has this person ever discipled another person?
12. How would you rate this person's spiritual maturity (Almost no maturity, some maturity, mature believer)?
13. Please enter any comments or observations about this person.

D. Collective Church Qualitative Assessment

1. Does your overall qualitative assessment match the church's metrics of healthy originally recorded in GAPP (the tracking tool "Gospel to All Peoples and Places")?

CPM Assessment Questionnaire

2. Does your overall qualitative assessment indicate this is a church or group?
3. If a church ... based on your interviews of individuals in this church, do you believe this is a healthy church meeting the 12 characteristics of health found in *Foundations* (the IMB's publication describing healthy church characteristics)?
4. If not fully healthy, which of the 12 characteristics are they meeting? (Select all that apply.)
5. Were you able to conduct a qualitative interview with the pastor, leader, or elder of this church?
6. If not, why?
7. Please enter any other comments or observations about this church.

APPENDIX D

SEVEN STAGES OF THE CPM CONTINUUM

The original authorship of the Seven-Stages is unknown and likely evolved over time with many contributors. The edition presented here was shared with me by Dave Coles in 2022.

0–CPM Team in context but no purposeful CPM plan or efforts yet

1–Moving purposefully–Trying to consistently establish 1st generation of *NEW* believers & churches

    1.1 Purposeful CPM Strategy (entry–looking for person of peace / houses of peace–and evangelism) **activity but no results yet**

    1.2 Have some *new* Gen1 believers

    1.3 Have some *new* Gen1 believers and *new* groups

    1.4 Have consistent *new* G1 believers

    1.5 Have consistent *new* G1 believers and *new* groups

    1.6 One or more *new* first-generation churches

    1.7 Several *new* G1 churches

1.8 G1 churches are starting new groups
1.9 Close to G2 churches (1+ G2 church)

2–**Focused**–Some 2nd gen churches (i.e. *new* believers/churches have started another generation)

3–**Breakthrough**–Consistent 2nd generation and some 3rd gen churches

4–**Emerging CPM**–Consistent 3rd gen churches and some 4th gen churches

5–**CPM**–consistent 4th^{++} generation churches in **multiple** streams

6–**Sustained CPM**–Visionary, indigenous leadership leading the movement with little/no need for outsiders. Stood test of time with at least several hundred churches (Most stage 6 CPMs have 1000 or more churches)

7–**Multiplying CPMs**–Initial CPM is now catalyzing other CPMs in other people groups or cities

Note: All generations counted are *new* believers and *new* groups/churches, not *existing* believers and churches. Existing believers/churches are labeled **Gen 0,** indicating that they are the baseline generation we are launching from.

BIBLIOGRAPHY

Books

Addison, Steve. *Movements that Change the World*. InterVarsity Press, 2011.

———. *What Jesus Started*. InterVarsity Press, 2012.

———. *Pioneering Movements*. 100 Movements, 2015.

———. *The Rise and Fall of Movements*. 100 Movements, 2019.

———. *Your Part in God's Story*. 100 Movements, 2021.

———. *Acts and the Movements of God*. 100 Movements, 2023.

Allen, Roland. *Missionary Methods: St. Paul's or St. Ours?* 1912; reissue, CreateSpace, 2018.

———. *The Spontaneous Expansion of the Church*. Lutterworth Press, 1927.

Anderson, Cynthia. *The Multiplier's Mindset: Thinking Differently About Discipleship*. DMMs Frontier Missions, 2023.

Barrett, David. *World Christian Encyclopedia*. Oxford University Press, 1982.

———. *Seven Hundred Plans to Evangelize the World*. New Hope Press, 1988.

Bevins, Winfield. *Marks of a Movement: What the Church Today Can Learn from the Wesleyan Revival*. Zondervan Reflective, 2019.

Bibliography

Carlton, Bruce. *An Analysis of the Impact of the Non-Residential Strategy Coordinator's Role in Southern Baptist Missiology,* DTh diss., University of South Africa, 2006.

Choudhrie, Victor. *Greet the Church in Your House.* Kindle Scribe, 2012.

Cooper, Michael T. *Ephesiology: A Study of the Ephesian Movement.* William Carey Library, 2020.

Davis, D. Ray. *Paradigm Shift in Missions: A History of Jerry Rankin's Leadership to Embrace Southern Baptist Churches in the Great Commission Task,* diss., Southeastern Baptist Theological Seminary, 2011.

Fielding, Charles, MD. *Preach and Heal, a Biblical Model for Missions* International Mission Board, SBC, 2008.

Garrison, David. *A Wind in the House of Islam.* WIGTake Resources, 2014.

———. *Church Planting Movements* booklet. International Mission Board, SBC, 1999.

———. *Church Planting Movements: How God Is Redeeming a Lost World.* WIGTake Resources, 2004.

———. *Strategic Directions for the 21st Century.* International Mission Board, SBC, 1997. Originally published as *Something New Under the Sun.*

———. *The Nonresidential Missionary.* MARC, 1990.

Gladwell, Malcolm. *The Tipping Point.* Little, Brown, and Co., 2006.

Greeson, Kevin. *Sowing with Intent: Jesus's Galilean Harvest Movement as a Model for Missions.* Dorrance, 2025.

———. *The Camel: How Muslims Are Coming to Faith in Christ!* WIGTake Resources, 2010.

———. *Developing a Strategy Using Jesus's Parable of the Sower for Entering New Ministry Areas.* diss., Southeastern Baptist Theological Seminary, 2021.

Hirsch, Alan. *The Forgotten Ways: Reactivating Apostolic Movements*. Brazos Press, 2006.

Ho, Peifeng Mary Tzen. *The Inverted Donut, the Lattice, and the Starfish: Designing the Organizational Architecture for All Nations*. PhD diss., Regent University, 2016.

Hogan, Brian. *There's a Sheep in My Bathtub: Birth of a Mongolian Church Planting Movement*. Asteroidea Books, 2017.

John, Victor, with Dave Coles. *Bhojpuri Breakthrough: A Movement that Keeps Multiplying*. WIGTake Resources, 2019.

Johnson, Todd, and Brian Grim. *The World's Religions in Figures*. Wiley-Blackwell, 2013.

Kai, Ying, and Grace Kai. *Ying and Grace Kai's Training for Trainers*. WIGTake Resources, 2018.

Lafferty, Todd. *Developing Pastors and Teachers within the Five-Fold Framework of Ephesians 4:11 to Sustain Church Planting Movements*. PhD diss., Malaysia Baptist Theological Seminary, 2020.

Larsen, Trevor. *Focus on Fruit! Movement Case Studies and Fruitful Practices*. Published by the author, 2018.

Lucas, Doug. *More Disciples: A Guide to Becoming and Multiplying Followers of Jesus*. WIGTake Resources, 2011.

McGavran, Donald. *The Bridges of God*. (World Dominion Press, 1955; reissue, Wipf and Stock, 2005.

Nyman, James. *Stubborn Perseverance*. Mission Network, 2017.

Ott, Craig, and Gene Wilson. *Global Church Planting: Biblical Principles and Best Practices for Multiplication*. Baker Academic, 2011.

Pratt, Zane, ed. *Foundations*. International Mission Board, SBC, 2018.

Prinz, Emanuel. *Movement Catalysts: Profile of an Apostolic Leader*. Published by the author, 2022.

Roberts Jr., Bob. *The Multiplying Church: The New Math for Starting New Churches*. Zondervan, 2008.

Schattner, Frank. *Sustainability Within Church-Planting Movements in East Asia,* diss., Cook School of Intercultural Studies, Biola University, May 2013.

———. *The Wheel Model: Catalyzing Sustainable Church Multiplication Movements.* Jessup Press, 2014.

Schindler, Dietrich G. *Creating and Sustaining a Church Planting Multiplication Movement in Germany,* diss., School of Theology, Fuller Theological Seminary, April 2006.

Shipman, Mike. *Any 3: Anyone, Anywhere, Anytime.* WIGTake Resources, 2013.

Sinclair, Daniel. *A Vision of the Possible: Pioneer Church Planting in Teams.* Published by the author, Authentic, 2006.

Smith, Steve, with Ying Kai. *T4T: A Discipleship Re-Revolution.* WIGTake Resources, 2011.

———. *An Evaluation of Training for Trainers (T4T) as an Aid for Developing Sustained Church Planting Movements (CPMs).* diss., University of South Africa, 2014.

Sutter, K. *Keys to Church Planting Movements.* Asteroidea Books, 2008.

Tasse, Aila, with Dave Coles. *Cabbages in the Desert: How God Transformed a Devout Muslim and Catalyzed Disciple Making Movements Among Unreached Peoples.* Beyond, 2024.

Thompson, David N. *Propelling a Movement of Multiplying Churches from the Summit Church in Raleigh-Durham, North Carolina,* DMin diss., Southeastern Baptist Theological Seminary, May 2014.

Trousdale, Jerry. *Miraculous Movements.* Thomas Nelson, 2012.

Trousdale, Jerry, and Glenn Sunshine. *The Kingdom Unleashed.* DMM Library, 2018.

Urbanek, Kurt. *An Analysis of the Ongoing Church Planting Movement among Western and Eastern Cuban Baptist*

Conventions from 1990–2008, PhD diss., Southeastern Baptist Theological Seminary, 2010.

———. *Cuba's Great Awakening*. Church Starting Network, 2012.

Warrick, Farah, ed. *Motus Dei, The Movement of God to Disciple the Nations*. William Carey Library, 2021.

Watson, David, and Paul Watson. *Contagious Disciple Making: Leading Others on a Journey of Discovery*. Thomas Nelson, 2014.

Zurlo, Gina, and Todd Johnson. *World Christian Encyclopedia, 3rd edition*. Edinburgh University Press, 2019.

Journals and Periodicals

Anderson, C. "In Serious Pursuit of Movements." *Mission Frontiers* (July 1, 2022).

Anonymous. "Any 3." *Mission Frontiers* (July 1, 2013).

Arlund, Pam. "Church-Planting Movements Among Oral Learners." *Mission Frontiers* (November 1, 2013).

Butler, Robby. "Reproducing Fishers of Men." *Mission Frontiers* (May 1, 2012).

———. "Church Planting Movements from One Indian Perspective." *Mission Frontiers* (March 1, 2011).

Carr, Chris. "House Church Planting in Bashkortostan, Russia." *Asian Missions Advance* 77 (Fall 2022): 27–30.

Cole, Neil. "Are There Church Planting Movements in North America?" *Mission Frontiers*. (March 1, 2011).

Coles, Dave, and Stan Parks. "24:14 Goal: Movement Engagement in Every Unreached People and Place by 2025." *Mission Frontiers* (November 1, 2019).

Esler, Ted. "Two Church Planting Paradigms." *International Journal of Frontier Missions*. (Summer 2013).

Bibliography

Fanning, Don. "Church Planting Movements." *Trends and Issues in Mission* 6 (2009). Accessed August 7, 2024. https://digital-commons.liberty.edu/cgm_missions/6/.

Farah, Warrick. "The Motus Dei Network: Fostering Communal Intelligence on Movements." *Mission Frontiers* (March 1, 2021).

⸻. "Identifying Current Gaps in Church Planting Movements Research: Integrating First-and Second-Order Perspectives." *Great Commission Research Journal* 13 (2): 21–36.

⸻. "The genesis and evolution of church-planting movements missiology." *Missiology: An International Review* 50:4 (May 24, 2022).

⸻. "The Homophilous Unit Paradox: Church Planting Movements Within and Beyond the Oikos." *International Journal of Frontier Missiology* 40:1–2 (Summer 2023).

Galanos, Chris. "From Big to Small—for a Big Movement." *Mission Frontiers* (January 1, 2020).

Garrison, David. "An Unexpected New Strategy: Using Nonresidential Missions to Finish the Task." *International Journal of Frontier Missions* (October, 1990).

⸻. "A New Model for Missions." *International Journal of Frontier Missions* (April 1992).

⸻. "Church Planting Movements." *Mission Frontiers* (March 1, 2000).

⸻. "Church Planting Movements vs. Insider Movements." *International Journal of Frontier Missions*" (Winter 2004).

⸻. "How to Kill a Church Planting Movement." in *Mission Frontiers* (November 1, 2004).

⸻. "10 Church Planting Movement FAQs." *Mission Frontiers* (March 1, 2011).

⸻. "God is Doing Something Historic." *Mission Frontiers* (January 1, 2013).

———. "God is Using Movements." *Mission Frontiers* (January 1, 2018).

Garrison, David, and Bill Smith. "A Church Planting Movement Unfolding in Uganda." *Mission Frontiers* (March 1, 2011).

Goodman, Bob. "Are we ACCELERATING or INHIBITING Movements to Christ." *Mission Frontiers* (September 1, 2020).

Greeson, Kevin. "Church Planting Movements Among Muslim Peoples." *Mission Frontiers* (March 1, 2011).

———. "Finding 'Fourth-Soil' People: A Movement Case Study." *Mission Frontiers* (July 1, 2018).

———. "Finding 'Fourth-Soil' People: Jesus' Modus Operandi for Establishing a Movement." *Mission Frontiers* (July 1, 2018).

———. "Finding 'Fourth-Soil' People: Fourth-Soil Person or Person of Peace. *Mission Frontiers* (July 1, 2018).

———. "Finding 'Fourth-Soil' People: Pursuing Movements as Jesus Did." *Mission Frontiers* (July 1, 2018).

———. "Finding 'Fourth-Soil' People: American Context" *Mission Frontiers* (July 1, 2018).

———. "Finding 'Fourth-Soil' People: Modern Day Application Using the Parable of the Sower as a Field Guide." *Mission Frontiers* (July 1, 2018).

Handy, W. L. "Correlating the Nevius Method with Church Planting Movements: Early Korean Revivals as a Case Study." *Eleutheria* 2:1 (2012).

Haney, Jim. "Assessing Church Planting Movements." *Mission Frontiers* (March 1, 2011).

———. "Engaged Unreached People Group." *Mission Frontiers* (December 26, 2012).

———. "Hitting the Mark." *Mission Frontiers* (April 30, 2016).

Hibbert, Richard. "Missionary Facilitation of New Movements to Christ." *International Journal of Frontier Missions* (Winter 2012).

Bibliography

Keener, Chris, and Dave Foster. "A Mathematically Based Model of Disciple Making Movements." in *Global Missiology* 22, no. 1 (January 2025).

Lewis, Rebecca. "Strategizing for Church Planting Movements in the Muslim World." *International Journal of Frontier Missions* (Summer 2004).

Lim, David S. "God's Kingdom as Oikos Church Networks." *International Journal of Frontier Missions* (January-December, 2017).

Liverman, Jeff. "What Does It Mean to Effectively 'Engage' a People?" *Mission Frontiers* (November 1, 2006).

Lucas, Doug. "Discovering the Fruitful Practices of Movements" *Mission Frontiers* (November 1, 2017).

———. "Finishing the Task Helping Participants View New Movements with Clarity." *Mission Frontiers* (April 30, 2016).

Massey, J. D. "Wrinkling Time in the Missionary Task: A Theological Review of Church Planting Movements Methodology." *Southwestern Journal of Theology* 55:1 (Fall 2012).

Mims, Neil. "Strategy Coordinator—the Outside Catalyst." *Mission Frontiers* (November 1, 2022).

Mims, Neil, and Bill Smith. "Church Planting Movements: What Have We Learned?" *Mission Frontiers* (March 11, 2011).

Moran, Ray. "Mission Viruses That Can Kill Disciple Making Movements." *Mission Frontiers* (September 1, 2020).

Moses, D. B. "Church Planting Movements Among Hindu Peoples." *Mission Frontiers* (March 1, 2011).

Nelson, Kurt, and Bob Garrett. "A Church Planting Movement in Cuba?" *Mission Frontiers* (March 1, 2011).

Nyman, R. "Women Engaged in Church-Planting Movements Among UPGs." *Mission Frontiers* (December 31, 2014).

Parks, Stan. "What is a CPM?" *Mission Frontiers* 41:4 (July/August 2019).

Ralls, Jon, and Chris Casey. "Media to Movements—A 24:14 Panel Discussion." *Mission Frontiers* (September-October 2022).

Ridgeway, John. "Key Insights in Enabling Movements Among Hindu and Muslim Peoples." *Mission Frontiers* (March 1, 2019).

Roberts, Mary, and Curtis Sergeant. "Movements Responding to Crises." *Mission Frontiers* (October 31, 2023).

Sergeant, Curtis, Doug Lucas, and David Garrison. "Can Kingdom Movement Strategies Work in North America?" *Mission Frontiers* (January 1, 2021).

Shank, Nathan. "Generational Mapping: Tracking Elements of Church Planting in Church Planting Movements." *Mission Frontiers* (November 1, 2012).

Slack, Jim. "Just How Many Church Planting Movements Are There?" *Mission Frontiers* (March 1, 2011).

Smith, Steve. "The Bible on Church Planting Movements, Qualified to Lead?" *Mission Frontiers* (February 28, 2011).

———. "Kingdom Kernels." *Mission Frontiers* (November 1, 2018).

———. "The Beginning of the End?" *Mission Frontiers* (September 1, 2017).

———. "The Oikos Hammer—You and Your Household" *Mission Frontiers* (August 28, 2018).

Smith, Steve, and Steve Addison. "The Bible on Church Planting Movements." *Mission Frontiers* (February 28, 2011).

Smith, Steve, and Stan Parks. "T4T or DMM (DBS)?—Only God Can Start a Church-Planting Movement, Part 1 of 2." *Mission Frontiers* (January 1, 2015).

———. "The War That Finally Ends." *Mission Frontiers* (January 1, 2018).

Smith, William. "Can Short-Term Teams Foster Church-Planting Movements?" *Mission Frontiers* (January 1, 2012).

Sundell, Jeff. "4x4 Movements." *Mission Frontiers* (March 1, 2014).

Sundell, Jeff, and Garrett Lawrence. "Movements Multiplying Movements" *Mission Frontiers* (February 29, 2016).

Waterman, L. D. "Daring to Succeed." *Mission Frontiers* (July 1, 2019).

Wood, Rick. "The Long Wait is Over." *Mission Frontiers* (March 1, 2022).

———. "Our Organic Gospel and Kingdom: God Intends for Us to Multiply." *Mission Frontiers* (July 1, 2018).

———. "Rapidly Multiplying Churches." *Mission Frontiers* (March 1, 2011).

———. "Reaching People." *Mission Frontiers* (March 1, 2010).

Wu, Jackson. "There Are No Church Planting Movements in the Bible: Why Biblical Exegesis and Missiological Methods Cannot Be Separated." *Global Missiology* (October 2014).

INDEX

Symbols
9 Marks 20
2000 Baptist Faith and Message 8

A
Addison vi, 34, 149, 201, 209
Adivasi 68, 69, 70, 71, 72, 168, 169, 173
Africa xvii, 3, 36, 49, 54, 59, 63, 64, 105, 110, 111, 122, 125, 126, 127, 129, 144, 146, 147, 168, 202, 204
African 64, 65, 110, 111, 112, 113, 114, 116, 118, 119, 120, 121, 126, 168, 169
African Traditional Religion 113, 114, 119, 120
Anko 114, 115, 171
annual statistical report 4, 5, 8, 45, 46, 79, 109, 134, 137
Asia xvii, 3, 29, 31, 32, 56, 59, 86, 87, 91, 93, 96, 148, 168, 170, 171, 185
Asian 28, 31, 49, 69, 87, 95, 101, 168, 185, 205

B
Bangladesh 49, 51, 52, 104, 105, 107, 108, 168
Baptist 3, 8, 18, 19, 22, 28, 31, 32, 33, 37, 43, 44, 45, 47, 48, 49, 53, 54, 55, 56, 57, 59, 60, 61, 62, 63, 64, 67, 68, 69, 70, 71, 73, 75, 76, 78, 79, 80, 81, 90, 95, 126, 128, 143, 148, 169, 202, 203, 204, 205, 211
Barrett, David 30, 33, 53
Basara 72, 73, 74, 75, 172
Batu 76, 77, 78
Bengali 47, 48, 49, 103, 105, 168, 171, 172, 173
Berber xiv, 59, 63, 64, 65, 66, 68, 168, 169
Bhojpuri 30, 36, 41, 42, 43, 44, 45, 47, 168, 173, 203
Bhow 75, 76, 77, 78, 173
biblical 145, 154, 202, 203, 210
Brosh 119, 120, 171

C
C2NC 133, 134
Cambodia 34, 52, 53, 54, 55, 56, 57, 168
Cambodian 52, 53, 54, 55, 56, 57, 169
Carey, William 27, 42, 47, 146, 202, 205
Catalyst 208
Carlton, Bruce 56, 76
Church Planting Movement xiv, xv, 14, 15, 21, 23, 29, 31, 32, 34, 36, 37, 55, 56, 68, 72, 74, 75, 76, 78, 81, 86, 90, 92, 93, 94, 95, 97, 99, 102, 103, 107, 110, 116, 117, 120, 121, 128, 144, 153, 154, 157, 165, 167, 171, 172, 173, 179, 186, 203, 204, 206, 207, 208
cities 3, 35, 64, 67, 83, 84, 95, 101, 102, 106, 130, 131, 132, 173, 183, 184, 200
City 35, 84, 85, 86, 87, 88, 89, 90, 91, 92, 93, 94, 95, 147, 172, 187
Co City 93, 94, 95, 172

211

Index

Coles, Dave xv, 36, 199, 203, 204
Communist xiv, 59, 62, 63, 169
Confidential Report 191
Cooper, Michael T. vii, 148
CPM i, xv, 9, 13, 18, 19, 21, 24, 27, 29, 30, 31, 36, 37, 43, 55, 56, 57, 76, 77, 81, 86, 91, 92, 93, 98, 102, 106, 107, 115, 117, 123, 127, 132, 133, 137, 144, 146, 149, 150, 154, 156, 157, 158, 165, 166, 173, 174, 185, 186, 187, 188, 189, 190, 191, 193, 195, 197, 199, 200, 208
Creation to New Creation 133
critic 178
Critics of Rapid Multiplication 24
Cuba vi, 59, 60, 61, 62, 63, 169, 205, 208

D
Daimu 118, 119, 171
DBS 32, 209
Denominational Critics 18
Dever 19, 20
diaspora 35, 64, 68, 123, 130, 131, 132, 133, 138
Directory of North American Agencies 27
Disciple Making Movement 121, 146, 157
disciples i, iii, vi, viii, 6, 12, 18, 19, 20, 22, 24, 29, 43, 59, 85, 89, 90, 92, 95, 99, 113, 116, 118, 119, 122, 138, 146, 151, 152, 155, 156, 157, 168, 169, 170, 171, 172, 174, 177, 186, 194
Discovery Bible Studies 32, 114, 115, 118, 120, 151
DMM 7, 145, 157, 204, 209
DNA 21, 189

E
East Asia 4, 101, 147, 204
East Asian 4
ecclesiology 37, 63, 78, 85
Europe xvii, 28, 64
executive summary 63, 67, 72, 87, 89, 91, 98, 99, 100, 107, 164, 165

F
Fan Christian 117
Farah iii, 35, 146, 205, 206
Fielding 144, 145, 202
Foro 125, 126, 127, 128, 168, 170, 173
Foster, Dave 145, 208
Fox 69, 70

G
GAPP 142, 143, 196
Garrison, David ii, iii, iv, vi, vii, xviii, 34, 60, 130, 131, 144, 209
Geisler ii, xv, 35, 135, 193
GenMapper 142, 143
Global Research Department xv, 4, 5, 8, 9, 37, 44, 48, 49, 61, 70, 74, 79, 82, 97, 104, 126, 130, 134, 135, 137, 138, 152, 187, 193, 211
Gospel to All Peoples and Places 142, 143, 196
Greeson 34, 35, 48, 49, 50, 52, 104, 148, 151, 202, 207
Guatemala vi, 78, 81, 168, 169

H
Handbook 27, 28, 29
Haney 49, 97, 104, 107, 111, 112, 117, 121, 207
heresy 20, 22
heretical 18
Hindu iii, xiv, 42, 47, 48, 68, 72, 73, 75, 108, 125, 133, 134, 170, 208, 209
Hirsch, Alan i, 35, 36
Holste 43, 53
home worship 61, 62
houses of prayer 61, 62
Hyde 56, 57

I
IMB vii, xiv, xv, xvii, 3, 4, 5, 6, 7, 8, 9, 28, 30, 34, 37, 41, 42, 43, 44, 45, 47, 49, 50, 51, 53, 54, 61, 65, 69, 70, 71, 74, 76, 79, 80, 82, 83, 84, 86, 87, 88, 91, 93, 94, 95,

Index

97, 100, 101, 104, 105, 107, 108, 109, 110, 111, 121, 125, 126, 129, 130, 131, 133, 134, 135, 136, 137, 149, 185, 193, 197
informants 44, 49, 50, 51, 52, 55, 61, 65, 68, 72, 74, 77, 78, 80, 87, 88, 89, 92, 94, 99, 105, 107, 108, 112, 113, 114, 115, 116, 117, 118, 119, 120, 121, 128, 129, 131, 133, 135, 136, 157, 158, 159, 161, 162, 169, 172, 185, 186
Insider Movements xiii, 7, 206
International Mission Board ii, xiv, xvii, 3, 4, 6, 8, 9, 31, 32, 33, 37, 41, 61, 82, 96, 100, 101, 111, 125, 131, 134, 137, 143, 145, 168, 187, 193, 202, 203, 211
interviews 44, 45, 46, 49, 50, 61, 65, 66, 71, 74, 77, 80, 87, 91, 94, 98, 99, 100, 106, 107, 109, 112, 113, 117, 119, 127, 128, 131, 132, 135, 161, 162, 169, 170, 197
Islam 48, 51, 68, 110, 112, 113, 117, 130, 131, 132, 170, 202

J
JESUS Film 30, 64

K
Kai, Ying 32, 85, 95, 96, 97, 98, 99, 100, 101, 102, 151, 203, 204
Keener, Chris 145
Kekchi 78, 79, 80, 81, 82, 168, 169
Koinonia 108, 109, 110, 171
Koro 116, 117, 171
Kusho 120, 171

L
Landmarkist Critics 22
Latin America 4, 59
Latin American 4
lay-led 18, 19, 20, 57, 84, 95, 110, 113, 159
leadership 8, 20, 44, 45, 48, 54, 57, 62, 67, 70, 72, 74, 77, 78, 87, 94, 100, 108, 116, 121, 126, 128, 135, 137, 142, 143, 144, 188, 189, 190, 200

literacy 37, 72, 115
Lo City 88, 89, 90, 172

M
Megalopolis 95, 97, 173
methodology 34, 46, 57, 84, 88, 163, 186, 191
Middle East 105, 135, 142, 144, 146, 168
Ministry as Mission Critics 22
MovementCatalysts 111, 112, 113, 114, 115, 116, 118, 119, 121, 122, 171
multiplication xvii, 6, 9, 24, 47, 60, 82, 94, 95, 98, 113, 122, 133, 141, 172, 188, 190
Muslim iii, xiv, 15, 36, 42, 47, 48, 49, 50, 51, 52, 63, 64, 65, 103, 104, 105, 112, 114, 115, 116, 117, 118, 120, 121, 125, 126, 127, 130, 131, 133, 134, 169, 172, 173, 204, 207, 208, 209

N
non-movements 125, 171, 172
North American Mission Handbook 27

O
Olduwar 108, 109, 110, 171

P
Parks, Keith viii, xv, 33, 205, 208, 209
pattern 81, 87, 155
prayer 23, 42, 61, 62, 85, 88, 100, 110, 114, 115, 117, 118, 136, 144, 151, 163
Prinz, Emanuel 149, 203

Q
quality ii, vii, xvii, 21, 25, 38, 122, 136, 143, 144, 159, 161, 163, 173, 186
quantity xvii, 21, 25, 38, 143, 144, 159, 161, 163, 186
Quellestan 133, 134, 135, 136, 137, 168, 170, 174, 193
Questionnaire 159, 187, 193, 195, 197

213

Index

R
radio 64, 67, 68, 69, 73, 127, 130
rapid xviii, 6, 9, 24, 57, 60, 62, 70, 84, 88, 89, 98, 113, 133, 144, 157, 172, 188, 190
Reformation 19
Reformed 18, 19, 21, 28, 44, 127
research ii, iv, vii, xvii, 33, 37, 49, 54, 56, 60, 65, 80, 84, 108, 112, 115, 116, 119, 120, 126, 128, 135, 152, 157, 160, 161, 172, 183, 191

S
Sahel 110
Sergeant, Curtis 32, 33, 209
seminaries 18, 19, 147
seminary 18, 19, 62, 126, 147
Seminary Critics 18
Shank 35, 142, 209
Shistan 129, 130, 131, 132, 133
Shistani 131, 132, 133, 168, 170
Slack xv, 37, 38, 43, 46, 49, 54, 56, 57, 61, 65, 71, 72, 74, 75, 80, 126, 128, 129, 131, 132, 136, 185, 187, 189, 191, 209
Smith, Bill 31, 32, 33, 42, 48, 97, 207, 208
Smith x, 31, 32, 33, 34, 42, 48, 96, 97, 98, 105, 147, 204, 207, 208, 209
Sobay 114, 171
So City 90, 91, 92, 172
South Asia 4, 5, 14, 30, 32, 34, 36, 37, 44, 47, 71, 72, 73, 74, 75, 76, 104, 105, 108, 123, 133, 134, 135, 141, 142, 144, 168, 169, 171, 172, 179
South East Asian 5
Southeast Asia 4, 29, 34, 52, 54, 55, 127, 146
Southern Baptist Convention ii, vi, 3, 4, 8, 9, 28, 145, 187, 193, 202, 203

Strategy Coordinator 31, 32, 34, 42, 48, 53, 64, 65, 73, 74, 84, 86, 87, 88, 90, 93, 94, 104, 108, 109, 110, 118, 119, 149, 151, 202, 208
Subsa 110, 111, 112, 114, 115, 116, 118, 119, 120, 121, 171
Sub-Saharan Africa 111
syncretism 51, 72, 74, 100, 117, 119, 129

T
T4T 32, 84, 85, 87, 88, 89, 90, 92, 93, 94, 95, 96, 99, 100, 101, 105, 147, 151, 170, 186, 204, 209
Ta Ethni 142, 143
Terry 44, 69
The Proclaimer 115, 118
Training for Trainers 32, 84, 96, 101, 102, 147, 151, 186, 203, 204
tribal 68, 72, 75, 169
trustee 4, 137, 170

U
urban iii, xiv, xv, 37, 42, 65, 68, 77, 82, 83, 84, 87, 88, 93, 95, 97, 98, 102, 109, 149, 150, 157, 159, 160, 163, 168, 169, 172, 183, 185, 186

W
Walu 113, 114, 171
Watt, Eric 35
Why So Remote 25
Wu City 84, 85, 86, 87, 172

Y
Yani 115, 116, 171

ACKNOWLEDGMENTS

Many generous contributors have made this book possible. First on the list is the Southern Baptist International Mission Board's Global Research Department. While a few other agencies and individuals are named within the book itself, others must remain anonymous due to the threat of repercussions in the countries where their personnel serve. Still other contributors have passed away; yet their pioneering work is reflected in this book, and they are remembered with gratitude and reverence.

www.ingramcontent.com/pod-product-compliance
Lightning Source LLC
Chambersburg PA
CBHW020050170426
43199CB00009B/239